Supporting early learning
The way forward

Vicky Hurst
Jenefer Joseph

Open University Press
Buckingham · Philadelphia

Open University Press
Celtic Court
22 Ballmoor
Buckingham
MK18 1XW

email: enquiries@openup.co.uk
world wide web: http://www.openup.co.uk

and
325 Chestnut Street
Philadelphia, PA 19106, USA

First Published 1998
Reprinted 2000

A catalogue record of this book is available from the British Library

ISBN   0 335 19951 8 (hb)   0 335 19950 X (pb)

Library of Congress Cataloging-in-Publication Data
Hurst, Vicky, 1941–
     Supporting early learning – the way forward / Vicky Hurst, Jenefer Joseph.
        p. cm. – (Supporting early learning)
     Includes bibliographical references and index.
     ISBN 0-335-19951-8 (hardcover). – ISBN 0-335-19950-X (pbk.)
     1. Early childhood education.   2. Early childhood education – Curricula.
3. Early childhood education – Parent participation.   4. Learning, Psychology
of.   5. Child development.   I. Joseph, Jenefer, 1926–   . II. Title. III.
Series.
LB1139.23.H87   1998
372.21–dc21   97-26527
                                                                                       CIP

Typeset by Type Study, Scarborough
Printed in Great Britain by Biddles Ltd, www.biddles.co.uk

Supporting early
learning

**LEARNING
SUPPORT
SERVICES**

Please return
on or before
the last date
stamped below

City College
NORWICH

2 0 APR 2004

2 0 MAY 2004

1 0 SEP 2004
1 3 JUN 2005

0 6 OCT 2005

2 4 NOV 2005

1 5 DEC 2005

- 6 FEB 2006

2 2 MAR 2006
0 8 JUN 2006

23 NOV 2006

1 5 DEC 2006

1 7 MAY 2007

1 1 JUN 2007
- 4 JUL 2007

0 5 SEP 2007

0 9 NOV 2007

- 4 JUN 2008

- 3 NOV 2008

1 0 DEC 2008

3 0 JAN 2009

0 3 FEB 2009

2 5 APR 2009

0 4 JAN 2010

1 FEB 2010

2 5 MAR 2010

3 0 MAY 2012
2 2 NOV 2012

Supporting early learning

Series Editors: Vicky Hurst and Jenefer Joseph

The focus of this series is on improving the effectiveness of early education. Policy developments come and go, and difficult decisions are often forced on those with responsibility for young children's well-being. This series aims to help with these decisions by showing how developmental approaches to early education provide a sound and positive basis for learning.

Each book recognizes that children from birth to 6 years old have particular developmental needs. This applies just as much to the acquisition of subject knowledge, skills and understanding as to other educational goals such as social skills, attitudes and dispositions. The importance of providing a learning environment that is carefully planned to stimulate children's own active learning is also stressed.

Throughout the series, readers are encouraged to reflect on the education being offered to young children, through revisiting developmental principles and using them to analyse their observations of children. In this way, readers can evaluate ideas about the most effective ways of educating young children and develop strategies for approaching their practice in ways that offer every child a more appropriate education.

Published titles:

Bernadette Duffy: *Supporting Creativity and Imagination in the Early Years*
Leslie Hendy and Lucy Toon: *Supporting Drama and Role Play in the Early Years*
Vicky Hurst and Jenefer Joseph: *Supporting Early Learning – The Way Forward*
Linda Pound: *Supporting Mathematical Development in the Early Years*
Iram Siraj-Blatchford and Priscilla Clarke: *Supporting Identity, Diversity and Language in the Early Years*
John Siraj-Blatchford and Iain MacLeod-Brudenell: *Supporting Science, Design and Technology in the Early Years*
Marian Whitehead: *Supporting Language and Literacy Development in the Early Years*

To the children of today and tomorrow

Contents

Acknowledgements

We wish to thank the children, parents and staff of the Dorothy Gardner Nursery Centre, London, for allowing us to take the photographs on pp. ix, 8, 17, 27, 37, 62, 69 and 73.

We wish to thank the children, parents and staff at Oxhey Nursery School, Hertfordshire, for allowing us to take the photographs on pp. 50 and 80.

We wish to thank Alex, Pam, Sam and Steven Forward for the photograph on the frontispiece.

We would also like to thank Shona Mullen of Open University Press for her calm help, advice and support throughout this enterprise.

Preface

Active exploration leads to learning

This book is one of a series which will be of interest to all those who are concerned with the care and education of children from birth to 6 years old – childminders, teachers and other professionals in schools, those who work in playgroups, private and community nurseries and similar institutions; governors, providers and managers. We also speak to parents and carers, whose involvement is probably the most influential of all for children's learning and development.

Our focus is on improving the effectiveness of early education. Policy developments come and go, and difficult decisions are often forced on all those with responsibility for young children's well-being. We aim to help with these decisions by showing how developmental approaches to young children's education not only accord with our fundamental educational principles, but provide a positive and sound basis for learning.

Each book recognizes and demonstrates that children from birth to 6 years old have particular developmental learning needs, and that all those providing care and education for them would be wise to approach their work developmentally. This applies just as much to the acquisition of subject knowledge, skills and understanding, as to other educational goals such as social skills, attitudes and dispositions. In this series there are several volumes with a subject-based focus, and the main aim is to show how that can be introduced to young children within the framework of an integrated and developmentally appropriate curriculum, without losing its integrity as an area of knowledge in its own right. We also stress the importance of providing a learning environment which is carefully planned for children's own active learning.

Access for all children is fundamental to the provision of educational opportunity. We are concerned to emphasize anti-discriminatory approaches throughout, as well as the importance of recognizing that meeting special educational needs must be an integral purpose of curriculum development and planning. We see the role of play in learning as a central one, and one which also relates to all-round emotional, social and physical development. Play, along with other forms of active learning, is normally a natural point of access to the curriculum for each child at his or her particular stage and level of understanding. It is therefore an essential force in making for equal opportunities in learning, intrinsic as it is to all areas of development. We believe that these two aspects, play and equal opportunities, are so important that we not only highlight them in each volume in this series, but we also include separate volumes on them as well.

Throughout this series, we encourage readers to reflect on the education being offered to young children, through revisiting the developmental principles which most practitioners hold, and using them to analyse their observations of the children. In this way, readers can evaluate ideas about the most effective ways of educating young children, and develop strategies for approaching their practice in ways which exemplify their fundamental educational beliefs, and offer every child a more appropriate education.

The authors of each book in the series subscribe to the following set of principles for a developmental curriculum:

Principles for a developmental curriculum

- Each child is an individual and should be respected and treated as such.
- The early years are a period of development in their own right, and education of young children should be seen as a specialism with its own valid criteria of appropriate practice.
- The role of the educator of young children is to engage actively with what most concerns the child, and to support learning through these preoccupations.
- The educator has a responsibility to foster positive attitudes in children to both self and others, and to counter negative messages which children may have received.
- Each child's cultural and linguistic endowment is seen as the fundamental medium of learning.
- An anti-discriminatory approach is the basis of all respect-worthy education, and is essential as a criterion for a developmentally appropriate curriculum (DAC).
- All children should be offered equal opportunities to progress and develop, and should have equal access to good-quality provision. The concepts of multiculturalism and anti-racism are intrinsic to this whole educational approach.
- Partnership with parents should be given priority as the most effective means of ensuring coherence and continuity in children's experiences, and in the curriculum offered to them.
- A democratic perspective permeates education of good quality and is the basis of transactions between people.

Vicky Hurst and Jenefer Joseph

Introduction

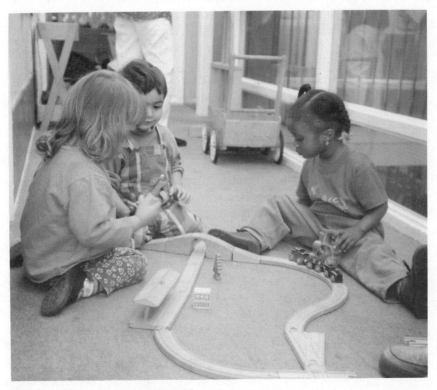

Learning to cooperate starts early in life

This book explores the neglected subject of the understanding of the developmental processes that lead to young children's understanding of themselves and of the world around them. The study of how children learn and how practitioners can best teach them has recently become unfashionable, yet this subject, pedagogy, can never be abolished, only neglected. Its displacement in favour of an orientation towards too strong an emphasis on the study of school subjects is the main cause of much inappropriate provision for early learning, and undermines academic and personal development alike. This chapter shows that if society is genuinely concerned to offer high quality to children, we must restore the necessity, for practitioners and policy makers alike, to acquire a sound understanding and knowledge of teaching and learning.

During the last 20 or 30 years, and in particular since the 1980s, there has been a plethora of research both here and overseas which indicates that extensive benefits are likely to come from the commitment of resources to discerning and judicious programmes of early years provision. And yet, for the greater part of this century, succeeding governments have been reluctant to promote the provision and expansion of early years education, and in particular nursery education, on two main grounds – that it is very expensive, and that not enough is known about its educational value to justify putting money into it.

The importance of the early years as a formative and foundational period in the life of us all has been well established. We now have a mass of hard evidence showing clearly how young children learn, what their needs and capabilities are, and the most appropriate ways of offering them educational experiences to match and enhance these. Furthermore, over the years there has been a significant addition to research evidence, which ought to have an immediate impact on both planning and the implementation of education and care for the under 2s (Trevarthen 1994). This evidence adds to the importance placed on the first six years of life, introducing as it does a new emphasis on the very youngest children, without diminishing the need for high standards of provision for children between 3 and 4, and between 5 and 6. It highlights the key factors in children's learning and development throughout the early years, shows that the learning of the youngest needs at least as careful attention as that of the 3s to 6s, and places in a fresh light established ideas about what is a suitable curriculum for all young children.

This body of evidence, which is constantly growing, confirms previous recognition that the years between birth and 6 are the foundation of children's physical, emotional and intellectual development for the rest of their lives. It adds to this a warning that the period between birth and the age of 2 is the most critical of all for children's development. Two areas are of particular concern: the development of the brain and the development of emotions. These mutually dependent aspects act in harmony to challenge, reinforce and extend one another in thinking and learning across the whole range of emotional, communicative, intellectual, physical, social, creative and moral growth. As brain development and the development of feelings are so deeply interconnected, damage or delay to one can result in difficulties for another, and this in turn can affect the whole development of a child.

Brierley (1988) drew attention to the importance of studies of the brain's development as a guide to how we should provide for education in early childhood. In 1994, the Carnegie Corporation of New York published the results of a wide-ranging review of research into all aspects of early childhood. These included research into the functioning and development of the brain from birth, and the influence of environmental factors on that development; the importance of family and community support during the first three years, and how the effects of these are evident as late as adolescence; the importance of the quality of the relationships between the child and its carers; and much else besides. We explore these in more depth in Chapter 1. As a result of the findings, the Carnegie Corporation issued a call for immediate action by all who could in any way contribute to improving provision for the youngest children. It was not just the statistics on poverty and the difficulties generally faced by parents that so concerned the writers. They also realized that neurological investigations of the development of the brain from birth onwards reveal that the permanent connections between parts of the brain, which are built up in the first two years of life, are more at risk during this period than was previously thought. It was believed until very recently that the brain's development was not particularly vulnerable in the early years, except to the effects of accidents, illness and malnutrition. This, it now seems, is not the case. The development of neurological connections during the first 24 months is dependent on receiving appropriate stimulation during this period. If this stimulation is not available, the connections will not be made, and are unlikely to be made later. There is, it seems, a critical period, rather like the critical periods for foetal development of limbs and organs, which provides a limited time for what is to take place. The connections established before the age of 2 will have to last the adult for the rest of his or her life.

These research findings also highlight the problems of poverty, lack of support and inadequate childcare experienced by many young families at this crucial stage. These difficulties are suspected of contributing to a lifelong failure, by children from the least affluent and most isolated families, to become successful achievers. This was reinforced by the generally poor quality of provision for the care and education of the youngest children. The report shows that children who receive inadequate or barely adequate care are 'more likely later to feel insecure with teachers, to distrust other children, and to face possible later rejection by other children. . . [This latter] appears to be a powerful predictor of unhappy results, including early dropping out of school and delinquency' (Carnegie Corporation of New York 1994: 49). Moreover, the financial cost of society's neglect runs into millions of dollars in dealing with remediation rather than preventative programmes.

These factors should be highlighted world-wide for their significance. They emphasize the need for training, advice, support and professional development opportunities at all levels. There are particular difficulties for staff working in group settings with children who are so young that they must be able to establish a close personal relationship through which to live and learn if they are to thrive. There is a great need for support for such staff (Miller *et al.* 1989), as well as guidance on how to assist staff in providing the warm and close relationships within which the youngest children can flourish and learn. Together, these factors will significantly enhance many children's chances of enjoying a warm, consistent, stimulating and satisfying learning environment which can capture their interest and motivate them to learn.

There is therefore no reason to doubt that investment in young children, and in training and support for the practitioners who work with them, would be wise. We need adaptable, creative, innovative and collaborative people who are good communicators. The kind of curriculum that enhances these qualities is described in Chapter 3.

It is ironic that the research evidence described has been largely ignored by those who are responsible for policy in education, and that developments in early years education and care have instead been driven by political expediency and ideology, to the detriment, by and large, of both the children involved and the adults working with them. For example, one of the major developments was the institution of the National Curriculum as part of the Education Reform Act 1988 (DES 1988). During the so-called 'consultation' period, the Secretary of State received many warnings about the possible adverse effects of establishing a National Curriculum, not least about the threat it would pose to children of 5 and under. Sadly, these warnings have proved to be true, and there has been a clear trickle-down effect on under-5 provision.

Perhaps the most unfortunate phenomenon of all has been the policy of allowing schools to admit children to infant school reception classes during the year after their fourth birthday. We now have (DfE 1993) over 80 per cent of 4-year-olds (often euphemistically called 'rising fives') in largely unsatisfactory conditions in reception classes of over 30 children. As Joseph says (1993: 10),

> Based on this, it is reasonable to say that four is now the unofficially acknowledged and accepted age at which children start formal schooling in England and Wales. This makes us unenviably unique in the world, five, six and even seven being the norm in other countries.

It also means that children in Britain now normally start school a whole two years earlier than children in the rest of the world, at a time when two years represents half their lifespan. Moreover, this is already having an adverse effect on established under-5 provision, as there are now only 3-year-olds in many settings, unable to enjoy the richness of interaction with the more experienced 4s, and losing the benefits of the family grouping which is of such profound importance for the welfare and development of very young children. In addition, the 4-year-olds in the reception classes are no longer the more experienced children in the group, to be looked up to, but have become the 'babies' of the class, losing status, competence and self-esteem.

Again, in spite of the fact that a wide cross-section of those working with young children believe that such matters as 'outcomes' and 'baseline assessment' are not appropriate for the under-5s, *Desirable Outcomes of Children's Learning on Entering Compulsory Education* was introduced in 1996 by the School Curriculum and Assessment Authority (SCAA) and the Department for Education and Employment (DfE). 'Outcomes' fit in with the ideology which considers test performance as being the only true evidence of children's progress, and which sees 'baseline assessment' at 4 as being necessary to know 'where the child is at' – but, of course, only in test performance in those aspects specified by SCAA (subsequently the Qualifications and Curriculum Agency (QCA)).

The introduction of the Voucher System for nursery children (1996) was resisted by many adults working with young children. They also pointed out that it was unlikely to succeed in raising standards because no money had been allocated for appropriate training. And yet the ideology, clearly exemplified by Lawlor (1994), which at root had the desire to get nursery provision mainly into private hands and away from local education authorities, ignored those at the grassroots level and forced vouchers onto an unwilling public.

There is an incredible diversity of provision for children from birth to 6, which has been allowed to grow and flourish, and which needs to be supported and well-coordinated within a planned structure. At present, children under statutory school age can attend a nursery school, nursery class, nursery centre, a childminder's premises, a playgroup, a day nursery

– or, as in many cases, a combination of two or more. What is more, in accommodating this wide diversity of provision, factors such as the requisite amount of indoor and outdoor space per child and, even more damagingly, the adult:child ratio have been de-regulated. This situation exists almost uniquely in Britain, and has a great deal to do with political expediency, which is happy to avoid financial expenditure and prefers to encourage charities, volunteers and others to provide the necessary education and care, without the requisite training and support. It also has much to do with the fact that no government to date has believed sufficiently in the fundamental importance of the early years to be concerned to 'do the right thing by young children'. In other words, there has been neither the conviction nor the will to do more than continue with the status quo.

This lack of will is disconcerting to say the least. It is an irrefutable fact that every adult has had a childhood; that they have memories of that time; and that they know that it has powerfully affected the way they have developed and the kind of adults they have become. And yet the politicians continue to ignore their own insights and the considerable evidence from research about the seminal importance of the early years, and demand instead some sort of 'proof' of its effectiveness.

Last but not least is the fact that the study of child development in teacher training courses has virtually disappeared in favour of 'subject' study. This leaves our young teachers, who are expected to provide leadership in curriculum development, with a very superficial knowledge and understanding of how young children learn, what their needs and capabilities are, and so on. As a consequence of the various factors discussed above, practitioners not only face tremendous pressures to conform to the resulting demands, but at the same time feel frustrated because they are being forced to lose sight of, or abandon, the principles about early childhood education which they continue to believe in, but which become harder and harder to maintain in their practice.

If one is pulled every which way, and both one's beliefs and one's practices are being threatened, what is the best way to deal with this? We believe that the surest way to stay on course is to begin by revisiting and updating one's educational theory about children's learning and development; hopefully to be reassured and strengthened by such a procedure; and then to look again at one's practice with a fresh eye and renewed vigour at the same time not being deflected by edicts from the powers that be, which too often, we suggest, have little to do with the provision of quality education.

This book takes the reader through this process. We show how the adoption of a developmental approach to young children's education not only accords with fundamental educational principles, but is a positive and sound basis for learning. We demonstrate that children from birth to 6 have particular developmental needs, and that all those providing care and education for them would be wise to approach their work developmentally. This applies just as much to the acquisition of subject knowledge as to other educational goals such as social skills, attitudes and dispositions. It implies an *integrated* curriculum, and carefully planned learning environments, in and out of doors.

Access for all children is fundamental if there is to be true educational opportunity available. We emphasize anti-discriminatory and multicultural approaches throughout, as well as the importance of meeting special educational needs. We show how these procedures in the earliest stages of education offer the soundest foundation for social and moral development, and are an essential preparation for later participation in democratic processes.

Play is normally a natural point of access to the curriculum for each child at his or her particular stage and level of understanding. We show how it is therefore an essential element in offering equal opportunities in learning, relating as it does to all-round emotional, social, intellectual and physical development.

Finally, we remind readers of the educational principles, spelt out in the Preface, to which we subscribe, and which underpin our approach to early years education.

We believe that what we have to offer will be of relevance to everyone working in the variety of situations mentioned earlier, and will serve to re-enthuse them, and to reinforce the fact that the work they do is of crucial importance both to the children in their care, and to society as a whole.

1

Children learning

How high can I make this?

Human relationships are highly complex, and each of us carries our own accumulation of beliefs, concerns and preoccupations. We need to think about the processes which have led us to become as we are, and this means having a well-informed understanding of how children build up a picture of themselves, the world and their place in it. We need to be aware, for example, that it is through our own actions and responses that we teach children how to value themselves and each other. If we do not have this understanding, or if we have it but come to believe that other things are more important in education, there is a risk that children's needs – emotional, physical, social, communicative and intellectual – will be over-looked. This will have an immediate and long-term effect on their feelings about themselves and others, and on their attitudes to learning.

Practitioners also need more detailed guidance which will make it poss-ible to apply theoretical understanding to real-life situations. Clear state-ments about how children learn should be the starting point of every curriculum and all educational arrangements for young children. Again, as decisions are taken and plans made, it is important to show how prin-ciples of children's learning justify what is being done. What we are talk-ing about here is the reinstatement of pedagogy as the main criterion for ensuring that children's most vital needs are taken into account, and for achieving quality in our educational practice.

Unfortunately, in the rush to condemn 'woolly' theory, the educational reforms of the 1980s and 1990s jettisoned acknowledging how children learn as a precondition for curriculum proposals. The Programmes of Study of the National Curriculum, and the subject area statements of the *Desirable Outcomes for Children's Learning on Entering Compulsory Education* (SCAA 1996), gave the impression that the content to be learned could be separated from the methods by which it is taught. This is not the case. In every decision about education, there is a model of learning and teaching involved. The model that was intrinsic to SCAA's thinking and to the National Curriculum was that children learn mainly by being told, and that they learn within the framework of subject areas. Hence the emphasis on whole-group instruction and on assessment of subject-based know-ledge, understanding and skills. However, the principles of learning and teaching that underpin what practitioners do are omitted in both of these documents – perhaps to avoid having to enter into discussion of theory which would acknowledge their vital place in every reasoned act in edu-cation.

This silence on the key subject of pedagogy brings serious additional problems. First, it causes two of the most important groups who are responsible for children's welfare – parents and governors – to be uncertain whether it matters if practitioners know how children learn.

This means that they are less likely to ask for the educational justification of decisions, or to seek opportunities to talk through with practitioners what the implications of such decisions might be. Moreover, lack of recognition of the significance of pedagogy may make appointing bodies undervalue the importance of appropriate training and experience in candidates for early years work. Practitioners working with children under 6 are, in fact, already significantly disadvantaged in terms of their lack of appropriate training, as reported in the Principles into Practice project (Blenkin and Yue 1994).

A second problem is that this silence about pedagogy tends to draw attention away from the highly responsible and demanding nature of early childhood care and education. Very young children are so intimately dependent on adults for their learning and development that an effective practitioner must acquire great sensitivity in interpersonal relations as well as being able to understand the processes of human learning and the gradual structuring of human knowledge. To the uninformed eye, being sensitive to children's feelings, ideas, creativity, communications, friendships and choices can be mistaken for a lack of intellectual rigour. Again, an understanding of human learning, particularly with reference to play, can be mistaken for permissiveness and lack of commitment to academic goals. The understanding that it is largely through their own efforts and preoccupations that children build up their concepts of the world can be mistaken for a low-level engagement with simple ideas. As a result, and perhaps worst of all, the human and humane qualities which distinguish the early years curriculum at its best can be assumed to be non-educational when, instead, it is those curricula which do *not* have these qualities which fail the test.

The reasons that may lie behind these misconceptions, and what can be done about them, are explored later (pp. 86–90). Unfortunately, they reinforce the professional disadvantages of early years practitioners across the board. They are assigned a low status, and many of those who are not trained teachers work for derisory pay. The 'Mum's Army' initiative (DfE 1993), in which central government sought to allow unqualified people to teach the youngest pupils in infant schools, showed how little early education was understood at policy-making levels. The fact that those employed in the private sector cannot get time for in-service training prohibits their professional development. Playgroup workers have to finance all their own training, which, as the Pre-school Learning Alliance and other organizations in the field complain, is hardly conducive to improving their qualifications, particularly when they are poorly paid as well. Again, childminders in England have not been regarded as being able to meet the requirements of the Desirable Outcomes although in many ways home-based care and education offer plentiful opportunities. Childminders are also in the same difficulties over training as the practitioners mentioned above. The absence of a clear model of learning and teaching for the under-6s causes one more serious problem: it draws attention away from the most fruitful and obvious avenues for the improvement of provision in early learning – appropriate teacher-training courses. Since 1988, except for a few exceptional initiatives, courses leading to qualified teacher status have been almost completely restricted, by government regulation, to the study of the content and teaching of the required subjects in the National Curriculum. Moreover, in-service training under government funding has been denuded of age phase specialist courses.

The authors of this book believe that the reinstatement of the study of teaching and learning is of vital importance for all those involved in early education, whether they be practitioners or policy makers, administrators or trainers. We write from this fundamental base, and the discussion of how children learn and how educators teach is at the core of it. We believe that this focus is the way forward to supporting early learning of our title.

In this chapter, we discuss the various ways in which children learn during the years from birth to 6, and the factors which affect that learning. Together, these have given us a view of early childhood which has led us not only to the fundamental educational principles outlined in the Introduction, but also to believe that the Developmentally Appropriate Curriculum (DAC) is the best way to offer children a sound beginning to their educational and personal lives. This is discussed in full in Chapter 3.

It is in this century, more than any other, that understanding of how human beings grow and develop from birth has emerged. It is acknowledged that childhood is a time of life in its own right, with its own distinctive characteristics and attributes. It is accepted, too, that children have their unique ways of learning and of coming to understand themselves and the world about them. As we have said, the more adults recognize this, and acquaint themselves with the processes involved in children's learning and development, the more they can ensure that children are exposed to the wealth of experiences and interpersonal relationships which will nurture their early development. This century is peppered with the names of the psychologists, educationists and philosophers who have helped us all to understand children, and to formulate ideas of how best to provide for them. From Freud to Froebel; from Susan Isaacs to Piaget; from Erikson to Carl Rogers; from Vygotsky to Bruner; from Dewey to John Holt; from the McMillan sisters to John Brierley; from Gordon Wells to Ferre Laevers – all of these people, and many others, have contributed to our common knowledge of, and insight into, children's minds and hearts, so that today we have no excuse for not acting on their theories and perceptions.

What then is generally known about how children between birth and 6 learn and develop? This is a good moment to say that whatever the processes are, it is during this period of childhood that growth and development are at their most rapid. If we think of the amazing achievements of, say, a 3-year-old, we can see the truth of this. What is more, learning during these first six years is at its easiest, and also much of what is learned remains for life. We never really lose physical skills acquired during this time, like swimming or riding a bike; an accent or dialect first acquired when developing speech in the mother tongue is almost impossible to lose without severe speech training; and poems and rhymes learnt at home or school are seldom forgotten – think how easy it is to recite 'Humpty Dumpty' or 'Jack and Jill' in adulthood. It is because so many fundamental patterns of our future behaviour are so quickly and soundly laid that this period in our lives is so crucial.

The following are perhaps the most commonly agreed features of learning and development; they are the basis of the writers' own pedagogy, and have informed our comments and proposals in the rest of the book:

- Children learn best in social contexts, when they are interacting in meaningful ways with their peers or with adults.
- Children learn best through their earnest exploration of the world about them, actively constructing their own understanding of it.
- Children learn best through their own self-initiated play.
- Children learn holistically, and do not divide their thinking up into 'subjects'.
- Children's language development facilitates their learning at all levels.

These aspects will be discussed in detail; but underlying all discussion of development is the way in which the human brain functions, and we wish to consider this first. It is only in comparatively recent years that studies have been done on all-round development from birth onward, and the research has revealed startling evidence of competencies previously unrecognized (Brierley 1988; Trevarthen 1993, 1994; Goldschmied and Jackson 1994). Studies of the brain and the effect of the environment on it demonstrate how fundamental a part this plays in social, emotional and intellectual development. The Carnegie Corporation of New York (1994: 7–9) shows how this research points to five key findings:

1 *The brain development that takes place before age 1 is more rapid and extensive than we previously realized.*
  It is now known that whilst brain cell formation is virtually complete at birth, brain maturation is far from over.

The next challenge is the formation of connections among these cells, or synapses... which form the brain's physical 'maps' that allow learning to take place... In the months after birth this process proceeds with astounding rapidity, increasing from 50 trillion to 1000 trillion.

This is significant because the brain's capabilities for learning depend on the richness of this branching of nerve networks.

2 *Brain development is much more vulnerable to environmental influence than we ever suspected.*
We have long been aware of the fact that poor nutrition, both before and after birth, can 'so seriously interfere with brain development that it may lead to a host of neurological and behavioural disorders, including learning disabilities and mental retardation'. But since the 1960s, scientific researchers around the world have been producing evidence of how much more important the role of the whole environment is for the development of the brain than had been suspected. This is particularly so in relation to the amount and type of *stimulation* which the child receives, especially during the first 18 months of life when cognitive deficits may not be reversible. This is substantiated and taken further by Brierley (1988: 4), who maintains that brain growth includes

> a number of sensitive periods for the development of vital human attributes such as vision and speech. If these periods are neglected, the optimum time for the acquisition of skills and some attributes is passed, and they may never be so easily learned again: a bird learns to sing and to fly at the right time, but the process is slow and impaired once the critical stage has been passed unexploited.

3 *The influence of early environment on brain development is long-lasting.*
It is significant here to note that 'long-lasting' can mean until the age of 15 or more, suggesting that over time the benefits of early intervention are cumulative.

4 *The environment affects not only the number of brain cells and the number of connections among them, but also the way these connections are 'wired'.*
These refinements are particularly evident in the early years of life.

5 *We have new scientific evidence for the negative impact of early stress on brain function.*
This research 'provides a scientific basis for the long-recognized fact that children who have experienced extreme stress in their earliest years are at greater risk for developing a variety of cognitive, behavioural and

emotional difficulties'. Again, Brierley maintains that a poor and stress-ful environment cripples

> because a narrow environment, with shut-down answers to ques-
> tions, a prohibitive attitude to a child's natural instinct to explore,
> and little company or stimulus may permanently retard mental
> development, perhaps by altering in some way nerve connections.
> It will almost certainly lower self-esteem [ibid., p. 8].

These findings make it abundantly clear that the brain is significantly affected by the environment that very young children grow up in, and the types of experience they have. Clearly, if we wish to prevent damage to growing children, we must ensure that in these first years of life they are properly nurtured – physically, socially, emotionally and intellectually. Disadvantages in early life cast long dark shadows forward.

We return now to considering the main ways in which young children learn, and the role that adults can play.

Children learn best in social contexts, when they are interacting in meaningful ways with their peers or with adults

This can be observed almost from the moment of birth. We can see the obvious calm and satisfaction which a new baby shows when it is cradled in its mother's arms, and is contentedly suckling, and we can most cer-tainly hear the cries of frustration or rage if that comfort is not forthcom-ing. This is evidence not only of the physical nurturing which the baby is experiencing, but of the social and emotional interaction which is taking place between the baby and its prime carer. Trevarthen (1993: 70) demon-strates how babies come equipped with ideas about how the world could work: 'one of the difficulties of working with newborns is that they have minds of their own!' They know, for instance, whether they are being spoken to with affection or not – and this at only 20 minutes old. Where obvious warmth and love are being offered by a parent, observation shows manifestly positive and excited responses through the baby's facial expressions, and its vigorous arm and leg movements reaching out towards the parent. Again, watching a 10-week-old baby with his/her father, one can see, through the hands, faces, and voices of both indi-viduals, the intimacy, trust and companionship which have already been built up between them. These intimate beginnings are vital to the develop-ment of self-confidence and a positive self-concept, and Trevarthen shows clearly how the emotional well-being of very young children is also inextricably linked to their cognitive development. Learning has started.

We mentioned *trust* – an important factor which has significance not only during the early years, but throughout life. Children who in their early years learn to trust other people or even inanimate objects have a base of security from which they feel it is safe to venture forth to more challenging things. They develop the courage to indulge their natural curiosity, and explore and experiment, learning about the world as they do. In this way, they slowly become more autonomous, and begin to assert independence of mind and action. Erik Erikson (1963: 273) believed that the development of a 'sense of trust' was the foundation stone for a 'healthy' personality. He demonstrated that children brought up in emotionally unfavourable circumstances have less reason to trust the human race; are less likely to develop a sense of responsibility towards others; and are more likely to have subsequent mental problems. Erikson believed that it was only at about 3 months of age that the baby began to develop trust in those around him/her whereas, as we have seen, Trevarthen demonstrates that it begins from day one.

The relationships with other human beings which the baby has from birth are fundamental to early learning. This seems obvious when we observe, for example, the development of 'social niceties', such as the 2-year-old maturing from being almost totally egocentric to (even as soon as 3, and certainly at 4) being happy to share something or, of their own free will, to help someone else. How could the following incidents have taken place without the children having had considerable experience of the give and take of social relationships?

Observation 1

Two 4-year-old girls in the nursery school had taken themselves to the table, where a glass tank housed some live snails. There was a safety net over the top of the tank, which could easily be lifted to examine or remove the snails. There was also a magnifying glass available.

Tracy: [Picking up two snails] These ones are empty, they are.

Sally: Hold this up for me [the corner of the net]. Tracy complies. She peers in. Oh, look a baby one. It's just like the one in the pot. Look! [She compares them.] Look! Snap, snap, snap.

Tracy: I wonder if there's any beetles in there. Please give me that [the magnifying glass], I would like to have a look.

Sally: My turn now. I want to look at these beans [a tray of growing bean shoots at the side of the tank]). She takes the magnifier and examines the beans, with Tracy looking along with her. Ooh, that's a giant.

Tracy: Yes, it looks like peppermint.

Sally: Ooh yummy, let's eat them all up! [They both shriek with laughter at this, and run off to delight the teacher with their idea.]

Observation 2

David (4y.) has been pushing Ann (3y. 6m.) in a large truck, outside in the nursery grounds. David suddenly stops and runs off, leaving Ann stranded.

Ann: [calling out] Oh David, push me. PUSH me, David.

There being no response, Ann sits despondent for a moment, then tries to edge the truck forward with her body, but fails. At this point, Sarah (4y. 2m.), who has been sharing a tricycle with a friend, and who has seen the Ann incident, stops the bike and calls to Ann, 'Do you want me to push you?'

Ann: Yes.

Sarah abandons her friend, goes over to Ann, and as she starts pushing her, she calls out to friend: 'I'll see you later on when it's lunch time'. Then to Ann, 'Don't worry, it's all right now.'

Observation 3

Alex (4y. 4m.), was sitting with his father watching a TV news item of a small boy, in hospital, crying for his daddy. Alex, clearly moved and identifying with the boy, said to his father, 'I could send him my Action Man. That would cheer him up.'

The sharing, caring and altruism in these examples show how much the children have learned from their past interpersonal experiences, and how very well socialized they already are.

So much for social development. But what about intellectual or cognitive development? How does the social context impinge on this? Obviously the children's explorations, experimentations and representations continue to be the major driving forces in their learning and development. But there will be many times when the guidance of an adult who is alive to their needs will be of most help to their making headway. The ways in which adults interact with children will be informed by their understanding of children's developmental stages in all aspects of learning. Equally important is the knowledge they have of each individual child in their care, and the points they have reached in various situations, whether it be mathematical thinking, moral dilemmas, motor coordination or whatever. It is the combination of this knowledge and understanding which makes

It's as tall as me

it possible for the adult to help the child to move on, so that learning and ✓ development are enhanced.

Vygotsky has given us a particular insight into this aspect of promoting children's learning. He shows us that whilst learning and development are interwoven in a cyclical way, it is learning which has to take place first, and which leads to development. If we think back to Trevarthen's work with babies, it is obvious that the very first step the baby takes is to learn something, even if it is simply that the 'outside' world is a much noisier and brighter one than the 'inside' one. Some development follows, which in turn leads to more learning, then to more development and so on. The important thing is that 'learning and development are interrelated from the child's very first day of life' (Vygotsky 1978: 84). Vygotsky acknowledges that learning has to be matched in some way to the child's developmental level, but points out that we should not limit ourselves simply to determining the developmental levels, if we 'wish to discover the actual relations of the developmental *process* [our italics] to learning capabilities' (p. 85). There are at least two developmental levels – the *actual* developmental level, and the *proximal* or potential level. The actual level is to do with the child's mental functions as they are already established at a certain stage; the proximal level defines those functions that have not yet matured, but are in the process of maturation – 'functions that will mature tomorrow but are currently in an embryonic state' (p. 86). The Zone of Proximal Development (ZPD) is 'the distance between the actual developmental level as determined by independent problem solving, and the level of potential development, as determined through problem solving *under adult guidance or in collaboration with more capable peers*' (p. 86). In other words, the child can solve more advanced problems with the help of another, than he/she would on his/her own. The child in the ZPD displays his/her true level of mental development – and that is one which shows he/she is capable of functioning at a higher level than either the child or the adult had fully realized. Moreover, what is in the ZPD today will be the actual developmental level tomorrow – 'that is, what a child can do with assistance today she will be able to do by herself tomorrow' (p. 87), so continuing the spiral of learning and development.

The point about the adult's guidance here is the really telling one. Vygotsky is clear that the child needs the adult, not only to assess the actual level of his/her mental development, but to work with the child, suggesting, asking pertinent questions and so on, in order to help the child move into and through the ZPD. (This is a good place to say that we are using the term 'adult' here as shorthand; but it could be a parent, or a playgroup leader, a childminder or a teacher or a nursery nurse, or indeed an older sibling – in short, anyone who is more knowledgeable or skilled than the child.) We must also recognize that the long-established notion of 'matching' the child's level is insufficient. It is more like a first step in the process, and we need then to use our expertise to help the child to move on from where he/she is. Vygotsky says that this sort of matching is ineffective from the viewpoint of the child's overall development, because it is not aiming for a new stage of the developmental process but rather lags behind it. The notion of a ZPD enables us to maintain that 'the only "good learning" is that which is in advance of development' (p. 89). The adult's part in this gives us a clear indication that not only is the quality of our interaction with the child (especially on a one-to-one basis) of vital importance, but also that learning takes place in social contexts. This is indeed one of Vygotsky's strong arguments: 'learning awakens a variety of internal developmental processes that are able to operate only when the child is interacting with people in his environment, and in co-operation with his peers' (p. 90).

We move on now to considering the second main way in which young children learn.

Children learn best through their earnest exploration of the world about them, actively constructing their own understanding of it

Froebel (1887), Susan Isaacs (1960), Piaget (1966), Bruner (1977) and others have all asserted that active learning is a precondition for intellectual development, and anyone who has observed young children from birth to 6 knows full well how they seem to have an inner drive to actively explore the environments in which they find themselves. During the first two or three years of life, this probing is largely of a physically active nature, and parents especially have to be wary of open cupboards, knobs on TV and video sets, vases of flowers and so on. But of course it is through these investigations that children are learning. They are finding out about weight, texture, size, shape, sound, smell and taste; so whilst we need to protect children from danger, the more opportunities we can give them, especially before the age of 2, the better. Goldschmied and Jackson (1994: 89), when they give babies what they call a 'Treasure Basket' of a rich variety of everyday objects to explore, find that this can lead to astonishing lengths of concentration, and the beginnings of decision-making. 'We see the baby's intent observation, and her ability to choose and return to a favoured item . . . she is in no doubt about her ability to select and experiment'. They add that if children are to learn to make choices and decisions, whether simple or complex, 'they need appropriate opportunities for so doing from very early days – appropriate in the way choices relate to the stage they are at, and the amount of information they possess at the time' (Goldschmied and Jackson 1994: 90).

Being 'active' is often misunderstood to involve mere motor or physical involvement with the environment, and whilst this is sometimes true, it nearly always means much more than that. Active exploration involves bringing one's mind to bear on experiences, and interpreting them in relation to one's existing knowledge and understanding. It means trying to organize new information and knowledge into more coherent structures, so slowly building up concepts from life experiences, and interpreting their meaning. It is this interpretation of events, as much as the events themselves, which affects subsequent behaviour, and this is where the adult can play a vital role, helping the child to contemplate the meaning of the event.

Piaget (1966), perhaps more than anyone else, brought our attention to this notion of active exploration, and he showed how, through the mental processes of assimilation and accommodation, we continue throughout our lives to adapt our ideas and behaviour in the light of changing circumstances and information.

We should add that the more self-initiated the child's activities are, the more meaning they will have for the child, springing as they do from his/her own intentions and concepts. The following observation of a boy in a nursery unit is a good indication of this:

> Troy (3y. 10m.) had taken himself over to the corner of the room, where there was a large collection of lead farm animals, and some fences and trees. He sat down on the floor, and began separating the animals out into 'pens', the cows all together in one place, the pigs in another, and so on. He stayed at this self-initiated task for about ten minutes, and was sitting back, admiring his handiwork, when the teacher came up to him and started chatting with him about what he had been doing. At one stage, she picked up a horse from the horses' pen, and said:

> *Teacher:* Why didn't you put this one in with those? [indicating the cows]
>
> *Troy:* [After a moment's thought, picked up a cow, turned it over, and pointed to the udder] 'Because it hasn't got one of these!'

> This is a good example of a child using his powers of observation, and becoming involved, of his own volition, in mathematical classification.

Children learn best through their own self-initiated play

The importance of play in children's learning cannot be overestimated, and we devote a whole chapter to it (see Chapter 4). Suffice it to say here that Erikson, Piaget, Vygotsky and Bruner also had much to contribute on play, elucidating various aspects of it. Erikson (1963) and Piaget (1962) showed how, in play, the child's knowledge, experience and understanding are fused together, helping the child to come to terms with reality. Piaget also offered us a deeper appreciation of the function, in children's learning, of symbolic and imaginative play, especially if it is self-initiated and 'free' play. Bruner (1983) and Vygotsky (1962) both believed that play in the early years had considerable elements in it which served as a rehearsal for children's adult lives. Vygotsky went further, and felt that children, especially in their imaginative and free play, created their own ZPDs, so taking themselves further than their present developmental levels. 'In play a child is always above his average age, above his daily behaviour. In play it is as though he were a head taller than himself' (Vygotsky 1962: 102). The flow of free play, its meaning and significance for children's learning and all-round development, is expertly and thoroughly explored in Tina Bruce's work (1991).

It is important that we truly recognize that it is largely through the child's play that he/she develops scientific, mathematical, historical and geographical concepts. He/she also acquires social skills; develops imagination; learns the beginnings of respect for others' needs and rights; begins to develop a self-concept; increases powers of expression and communication, both in language and the arts; refines motor skills; and begins to acquire some notion of moral issues such as right and wrong, fairness and justice.

Children learn holistically, and do not divide their thinking up into 'subjects'

Perhaps this is best illustrated by example. The following is a transcription from a British Association for Early Childhood Education (BAECE, now Early Education) video made in 1994. It was recorded in a nursery school, and the observation lasted for five minutes.

Mandy, aged 4, on her own initiative, went over to the large wooden building blocks, and started making a construction on the floor. She carefully selected differing lengths of blocks, measuring them against each other in order to put together the structure she had in mind. After about three minutes, the teacher approached her, and the following conversation ensued:

Teacher: That looks interesting. What have you been making?

Mandy: Somewhere for the cars to go in.

Teacher: For the cars to go under? Why do they go under and not on the top?

Mandy: Because it's a tunnel, and when they [the cars] come, I have to let them through.

Teacher: Oh, so this is like a gate, is it, to open to let them come through?

Mandy: Yes.

Teacher: Do you know, when I was on holiday in a faraway place called Switzerland, we went through an incredibly long tunnel, through a mountain, in the car, and it took us absolutely ages, and there were no lights, just the lights of the car, so it was really dark. Is your tunnel very dark in there?

Mandy: [looking inside] Not that dark. I could put more blocks there, like a door.

Teacher: You could block it off. Yes. How could you tell if it was dark inside?

Mandy: You could take the top off [i.e. remove one of the blocks on top].

Teacher: Shall we build up the end then?

Mandy: Yes.

Teacher: What size bricks do we need?

Mandy: Very long ones.

Teacher: So you're going to match these with these? [i.e. long ones with long ones] How many do you think you'll need to build it up to there? [the top].

Mandy: [after a slight pause] Four.

Teacher: How do you know it'll be four?

Mandy: I can see.

What do we think the child has learned from this situation? She herself most certainly would not have compartmentalized her thinking in any way, but she was in fact thinking mathematically (measuring, matching, estimating); geographically (faraway Switzerland); she was involved in the beginnings of problem-solving (how could you tell if it was dark in there?); she was adding to her linguistic skills, by hearing the teacher use long and (possibly) unfamiliar words like 'incredibly' and 'absolutely'; her motor coordination was being applied; and all of this was in the context of a friendly one-to-one conversation, and arising out of the child's self-initiated play.

This is not only a good example of holistic learning, but also shows how a skilful and knowledgeable adult can recognize that that is what is happening, and help to take the child forward in his/her thinking and understanding. Moreover, it demonstrates that for young children a 'subject-based' approach to a curriculum is inappropriate, as it goes against the ways in which children think and learn. The programmes of study in the present National Curriculum are divided into areas – art, geography, English, mathematics, physical education, science, information technology, and design and technology – and this goes against the grain of what we have been saying. On the other hand, the holistic way of learning *is* partly recognized within the National Curriculum. The notion of 'cross-curricular themes, dimensions and skills' subscribes to the fact that bringing different kinds of subject knowledge together can be the most fruitful way of promoting learning, and those practitioners who are involved with carrying out the NC would do their children a great favour if they made the most of that acknowledgement.

Children's language development facilitates their learning at all levels

There have been, and still are, many researchers into the miraculous way in which young children acquire language, and into the relationship between language and thought. We consider it 'miraculous' mainly because of the speed with which most young children acquire it and come to use it, by the time they are 3, in grammatically correct forms and for all sorts of uses – to question, direct, reflect, explain and so on.

It is because language development is so complex, and such a facilitator of all-round development, that practitioners working with children from babyhood onwards need to know as much as possible about it, not only by reading about it, but by constant and careful observation, listening, talking and recording.

One of the most important qualities which language gives us is the ability to think in a symbolic way. That is to say, we can use words to represent things, feelings and thoughts. Imagine how difficult it would be, without them, to get someone to understand that 'I want my mummy', or 'I feel sad.' It also means that children can recount incidents that have happened to them, share reflections on them and bring forth memories of them. In this way they build up their own personal histories and mythologies.

People who work with babies and under-3s know that children can make themselves understood with just one word, as early as 10 or 11 months. 'Da' can mean 'There's Daddy' or 'I want my Daddy' or 'Give this to Daddy.' It all depends on the context, and on how aware the adult is of that context, if the word is to be correctly interpreted. By the time the child is about 3, he/she can usually speak in grammatically correct sentences, using the past and the present tense (albeit with the odd 'mistake' like 'I goed', which in fact demonstrates understanding of how the past tense is formed); and between 3 and 6 there is a great leap forward, both in the amount of vocabulary being used, and in the sophistication of the use of language in general. Alex, aged 5, having watched the video of the stunning Riverdance dancers, said, 'Actually, I think the men were better than the women. They're neater!'

It is clear that a facility with language is a major factor in enhancing children's learning, and is of particular significance during these early years whilst the foundations of all later learning are being laid.

Two further important points need to be made. The first is to do with the fact that because our society is a multicultural, multiracial one, practitioners working with young children need to recognize that cultural differences are often reflected in child-rearing practices, and these have to be accommodated wherever and whenever possible and appropriate. Views on childhood, and on the best ways of bringing up children, are arrived at within each particular culture, and help to determine the common practices connected with gender, feeding and sleeping, encouragement (or not) of independence, discipline, the role of play in learning, and so on. Having said that, it should also be pointed out that even within the same culture there are differences of opinion about the best ways in which to rear children. For example, smacking children in schools, playgroups etc is no longer allowed, and yet there is still a considerable proportion of people in this country who call for corporal punishment to be reinstated even for very young children. People who voice their opinions on this subject may or may not be representative of the majority view, if there is one, of a particular culture.

Those of us working with young children need to be aware of these possible differences in values and beliefs, and to discuss them with the parents. They, after all, can give the clearest information and explanation of their preferred practices and, in discussion, practitioners have the opportunity to express and justify any differing view which they might hold. Together, better understanding all round will be gained – to the benefit of the child, the family and the setting. Moreover, whilst there may not be a sort of global blueprint for the 'right' ways to rear children, there would seem to be a universally shared belief in the importance of providing children with love and security within caring environments – even though the methods for achieving these may differ from culture to culture. So there is a great deal of common ground as well as divergence. This applies equally to how children learn – as we have shown in this chapter, research indicates that the processes of learning are universal.

Practitioners also need to keep themselves well informed, through courses and reading, about differing cultural beliefs and practices, so that they can draw on their richness and incorporate it throughout the curriculum. Again, the more parents are encouraged to take part in the setting's activities, the more they can enrich the children's learning with the diversity of resources and personal talents which they bring to it.

Secondly, it is important to say that everything which has been said so far applies equally to children with special educational needs. The processes of their learning are no different from that of other children. In fact, these children actually *demand* a holistic approach, as it is even more important that their own interests and pursuits should be the starting points for their learning. However, adults working with these children will naturally place different emphases on different aspects, dependent on the particular needs which a child may have. For example, it may be more helpful to a child with severe learning difficulties for the adult to more frequently take an initiatory role in order to stimulate learning; or for there to be many more imitative and repetitive activities than there would be with other children. But the processes of learning through play and exploration and experimentation apply equally.

By the time a child has turned 6, he/she has been a part of the living world for a mere 72 months. And yet the all-round development which is likely to have taken place during that brief time is formidable. With varying degress of success, he/she:

- can run, jump, skip, hop, balance, climb, dance;
- can be sympathetic, empathetic, helpful, kind, courageous;
- knows a great deal about what are 'good' things to do, and what are not, and has some understanding of fairness and justice;
- can represent his/her feelings and experiences creatively, through painting and modelling, telling and writing stories, drawing and constructing, dance and movement;
- uses language fluently, and for many purposes;
- may already be reading books, or well on the way to doing so;
- can reflect on his her own actions, recall past experiences, and predict consequences;
- has a good sense of self, and of self-respect.

The list is endless. The *processes* through which these accomplishments have been achieved not only include the types of adult/child interaction which have taken place, but have also come about through *play* with peers; through *communication* with children and adults involving speech and action; through *exploration, investigation and representation*; and through having the freedom to pursue *self-initiated activities* within the framework of secure and loving environments.

It is from all this that our own pedagogy has emerged; and this has led us to consider what might be the most suitable and appropriate ways, within a variety of settings, of putting our beliefs into practice. If children learn developmentally, a curriculum ought to be developmentally appropriate if it is to try to meet the needs of those children.

2

Personal and moral development

Children's self-respect grows from closeness to adults who love and value them as individuals

In Chapter 1 we described how children learn through their relationships with adults and other children, and how play, communication, movement, exploration and representation are the main ways in which children are active in their own learning. We drew attention to the processes of learning and highlighted them as very important. In addition to the outcomes of knowledge, understanding and skills, children are developing the attitudes and dispositions which will, or will not, make them into good citizens and lifelong self-motivated learners. We discussed early learning as holistic and compared it with the learning of separate school subjects, and we showed that many holistic understandings underpin subject learning and cross-subject learning. We described how early learning should be approached and we showed how, if it is well provided for in the years before 7, it can later become a sound foundation for the more formal learning that the school subjects require.

Too strong a pressure to achieve the goals of formal learning at this formative stage can in fact inhibit children's real understanding of the very ideas we are attempting to teach. However, this is not always appreciated, particularly by those who think of education as schooling in certain formal achievements. Here, two beliefs appear to be in conflict: the conviction that learning begins and develops informally is in conflict with the notion of learning being a formal process. In fact they are not in conflict, but they *are* different stages of the whole process of learning. In order to see how this comes about, and how the two stages can be dovetailed together, we consider one aspect of children's early learning that is prized very highly by parents and practitioners alike – the formation of positive attitudes.

Parents value the social experiences that group settings can offer, along with the opportunities to develop positive attitudes to oneself, to others, and to learning itself. These attitudes can have a powerful effect on children's future success as individuals and as members of society. Parents have the earliest influence, but other important adults also help to shape children's development. This means that everything a practitioner does and says has to be thought through from the perspective of how his or her own attitudes and dispositions are conveyed to children. This in turn challenges practitioners to think of the curriculum in terms of the experiences that children will have, as well as of intended subject content.

These experiences are the processes of learning (Blenkin and Kelly 1994), and they range from moral and social aspects to subjects such as science, history and the arts. Children learn from everything that happens to them. Even the practitioner's strategies for managing groups of children convey messages to them. For instance, having to queue up at the teacher's desk for long periods to ask how to spell a word does not encourage children to learn how to resolve their own problems.

In this chapter we emphasize one very important aspect of attitude formation: how to foster attitudes which lead to care of oneself, good relationships with others and self-discipline. These are valuable personal characteristics in themselves, and they also underpin learning. They are not the only attitudes that are essential for learning, but they are necessary if it is to take place. Understanding this guides us to the characteristics of an appropriate curriculum for young children's acquisition of desired attitudes. It illuminates how practitioners' understanding of general patterns of children's development and learning can be applied to their provision for individual children. It also helps us to identify some serious misconceptions that undermine attempts to improve educational achievement, and points to some possible ways to put these defects right.

Self-respect, self-discipline and respect for others

We argue here that the experiences of each child cause the development (or not) of these qualities. When the experiences are supportive of children's development they lead to positive attitudes, to feelings of being valued, and this helps children to develop self-respect. Respect for others follows from social experiences which suit children's developmental needs. Self-discipline follows from valuing oneself and others sufficiently to be able to shape behaviour to fit current challenges and demands. Children whose interests are respected will feel respect-worthy. They will be more able to respect other children's interests too, and will often be willing to share in them. They will be developing the self-discipline which enables them to put off their own concerns for a while in order to accommodate the differing intentions of their friends.

These are not only good emotional and social attitudes to have; they are essential for successful learning. Some of the most important qualities that make for being a good learner do not originate in the study of academic subjects. Self-doubt makes it hard for children to learn, as the battle is lost in advance; while optimism that one has the capacity to do things is encouraging to a learner. Valuing and respecting others' ways of doing things makes it easier to learn from and with others. Having the self-discipline to put aside some aims in order to achieve others that seem even more rewarding enables learners to persist even when there are difficulties. Inner qualities such as optimism that experiences will be enjoyable and successful; the self-confidence that one can achieve new understanding and skill; the courage to use one's imagination and think creatively in solving difficult problems; the perseverance to keep trying in the face of failure – these are general attitudes which, when grouped together, form powerful dispositions towards achievement. Understanding how this comes about opens up opportunities to create a curriculum that can provide for this development, without which all the other kinds of learning cannot take place successfully. Practitioners who recognize attitudes as being important aspects of learning can promote and enhance them through the approaches that they choose, using their knowledge of child development.

In Chapter 1 we set out the research which gives the clearest and best-supported guidance on how to provide for young children's learning and development. This research shows that, in the best conditions, development and learning go hand in hand and – as importantly – that feelings are essentially involved in learning. This is especially helpful when we consider attitudes, which develop over time, and are rooted in feelings as well as in intellectual understanding. It is the satisfaction of children's own needs which helps them to develop self-knowledge, self-respect and self-discipline. Parents are the first to meet these needs, and practitioners have the task of continuing what they have begun, but in different circumstances.

- Children's self-respect grows from closeness to adults who love and value them as individuals, enjoy their company and are stimulating companions. They acknowledge and support children's feelings while protecting them from danger and from hurting others.

- Children's self-knowledge and sense of self-value grow from being treated respectfully by others who know them well.

- Children's own growing self-respect and self-knowledge enable them to respond to others with understanding and respect.

- Respect for their own capacities as learners and for others as learners enables children to come to discipline themselves for their own educational and personal benefit.

The key concepts that are involved in the moral development necessary for self-discipline include the acceptance of differences between oneself and others and the empathetic capacity to imagine things from another's point of view. Respect is the key to all of this. Respect for oneself makes all the effort worthwhile and gives the hope that one can achieve good things; respect for others enables one to treat them as one would like to be treated; respect for learning and for oneself as a learner gives one the motivation and the self-confidence to struggle with difficulties.

Later in this chapter we describe an approach to providing for this kind of learning and development. First, however, it is important to note what is involved for children in leaving the home setting and entering into group learning. Cleave *et al.* (1982) found deep anxiety in children as they tried to find their way around the strange environment of the infant school. In an illuminating exploration of young children's experiences as they entered reception class at the age of four, Barrett (1986) drew on both parents' and practitioners' perspectives on the children. The practitioners saw them learning to become part of the group; the parents saw them at home, struggling to make sense of their feelings and to understand their experiences.

The children's feelings emanated from their experiences, their understandings about the new situation, the people they had met, the rules and requirements and, most puzzling of all, the differences in use of language. Laurie Lee (*Cider with Rosie*, 1964: 44) remembers his infant bewilderment at the teacher's way of using language; she told him to 'sit there and wait for the present', and he was distressed when he had to return home presentless. At home, language is negotiated between parent and child, and the child 'owns' it, at least to the extent of what is normally used between the partners in conversation (Tizard and Hughes 1984; Wells 1987). In group settings, people have different names and have roles unknown at home, such as 'key worker'; procedures, too, have unfamiliar names and have unknown rules attached to them, such as 'circle time'; and the language used is institutional, structured by tradition, by group or school culture, such as 'We're going to have P.E. in the hall and then we'll have assembly later, and we'll have choosing time after playtime.' Something is needed to help children to feel they can 'own' some of this bewildering new world, that they can make sense of it, that they have a place in it. Otherwise, they will hardly be able to survive with their self-confidence intact, let alone develop other qualities necessary for learning, such as the sense of mastery described by Dweck and Leggett (1988). When they venture into group settings it is vital that children are helped to retain their sense of themselves as valuable people, so as to enable them to develop the self-knowledge, self-respect, respect for others and self-discipline that we have been discussing.

We turn now to explore an example of how a sound knowledge of children's development can guide practitioners.

Stories, narratives and personal development

One of the main ways in which practitioners can enable children to bridge the gap between home and group settings is through the use of stories about the kinds of experience that children are having. These can be the children's own stories, the practitioner's own stories, picture-books or fairy-tales. The latter might not seem so relevant to modern children's experiences, but Bettelheim (1975) has shown how fairy-tales can give children support in their problems and guidance on the qualities they will need in life. Under the guise of distraction by wonder and enchantment, fairy-tales teach both moral and factual truths. The youngest son or daughter is often overlooked or despised, yet has the ability to achieve where other older people fail. It is often the apparently feeble creature, whether an old person or an animal, that holds the secret of success, and a wise youngster will give thoughtful attention to such as these. Courtesy, kindness, truthfulness and courage are worth more than gold.

These stories can be effective teachers because what children need to know is communicated through a medium which rivets their attention. Stories are the means by which humans have identified with the experiences of others throughout their changing history as a species, and children as well as adults are receptive to them and sensitive to their messages. It is not just the content, whether factual or fantastical, that is so powerful. Much attention has recently been directed to the role of stories in enabling children to make sense of their current experiences and to construct forecasts of what is likely to come. Grace Hallworth, the well-known storyteller, 'talks with great passion on the value – for all ages – of interactive storytelling. The experience of a story shared has the power to lift tensions, create understanding and to encourage individual expression, even among the very young' (Carey 1997: 5). Indeed, Piaget (1962) describes how his baby daughter Jacqueline recreated the story of bedtime through her body movements even before she had the verbal language to recount it.

Bettelheim has pointed to the content of fairy-tales as giving guidance; others have explored the structure of the story in itself as a learning medium. Stories help children to make connections between home and other settings (Egoff *et al.* 1980; Rosen 1988; Fox 1993; Zipes 1995; Whitehead 1996).

Behind the structure, the conventions, the 'storytelling voice' and the use of language, lies the whole idea of story as a personal communication that is shared and understood between people. Fox (1993) found that young children who had had plentiful experience of being read to were able to tell their own stories onto a tape. They had the picture of a story as conveying something the teller wanted to say and which the listener wanted to hear, in a form which was understood by both sides. The value of this communication for children is that it gives them a support for the thoughts and feelings that they want to express. Some children have this understanding so securely established that they can use it even when they cannot find the right vocabulary for what they want to say.

Grisha, aged 3 years 8 months, whose home language was Russian, spoke very little English. When he saw other children giving their 'news' in the group he stood up and announced 'And my Natasha, she is silly boy!', then beamed at everyone and sat down triumphantly.

Many children will not be as confident in a group as Grisha, and some thrive better in very small groups. Children whose care and education are provided by childminders usually find it much less daunting to speak out because the group is very small, the other children are well known, and a strong relationship has been established with the childminder. A group of Northamptonshire childminders commented that they felt they were in a favoured position to encourage children because they almost inevitably had close contact with the parent or parents. Regular exchanges of information about the children enabled them to understand and support children as they began to tell their stories about what interested them in their home life. The good adult-to-child ratio in settings governed by the Children Act 1989 helps practitioners in private nurseries, playgroups and after-school and play provision for older children to have this kind of supportive role as well; the same is true of maintained nursery education in nursery schools, centres and classes. In other settings, such as reception and Key Stage 1 classes, the ratios are much less good, and it must be harder for practitioners to help children tell their stories. It therefore becomes more important to plan for stories in the curriculum.

Children will always tell stories; from the first exchanges between newborn baby and parent, the dialogue stretches throughout childhood. Yet in a group setting they are much more likely to be able to contribute when their stories are valued, planned and provided for within the curriculum. ✓ All young children have stories to tell when the circumstances are right, and as the practitioner gets to know children and makes time and place for individuals' stories, the stories will be told. Paley (1981) is an example of a practitioner who has made stories the main medium of education in her classroom. Her study of one storytelling child in *Wally's Stories* shows her accepting and building on his contributions to find a way of understanding and helping him to find his place in the classroom and in the curriculum. Children's own stories help them to step into the group setting more confidently because they help them to feel they have a place there.

Storytelling with young children in a group setting is an art that has to be worked at. Stories have to be told face to face, as well as written and illustrated to be read at home and in the setting. Stories have to bring into the light aspects of the experiences and concerns of the participants in the setting. Paley herself tells of one more way in which story can be socially inclusive; she sets store by grandparents and parents as storytellers in her classroom because they can bring together on an equal footing the traditional tales and family histories that reflect the children's multicultural backgrounds.

Egan (1988) describes story as a primary means of understanding. It is a way of coming to know things about the world in itself; its demand for a logical structure of time, cause, motivation and so on makes it both intellectually challenging and, once mastered, a powerful tool for understanding. This draws our attention to the second quality of story that is so important for young learners – its imposition of coherence. A logical conclusion is that teaching should often be shaped as a story. Rosen's work (1988) with secondary children and with older primary groups has given details of how the structure of story enables children to develop ordered and meaningful ways to put their ideas and experiences into a form that can be conveyed to others. She herself has disclaimed experience with younger children, but the work of Fox (1993) makes it clear that both the challenge and the reward for the under-6s are great. Grace Hallworth reiterates this: 'Small children's powers of concentration are sadly underestimated. They aren't encouraged. It's too often assumed they have a short attention' (cited in Carey 1997: 5).

In fact, not only is story an important way of learning about the world, it also offers emotional security amid the many changes and uncertainties that children experience. There is much in children's lives that is incomprehensible, both in the language that adults use and in the constraints of the adult world. Children's lives are chopped up by restrictions of time, place and relationships they cannot understand; they often find it hard to forecast what will happen, and their grasp even of well-known adult-structured events is not well developed. Six- and seven-year-olds sometimes ask an adult whether they (the children) have had their school dinner yet. Their own stories give them a much-needed feeling of being in control and in this way they enhance their self-esteem and self-confidence. It is also essential that children should have experience both of telling their own stories and of listening to others' tales as part of the development of their capacity to put themselves in others' places; imagination needs the support of story to carry each child beyond the well-known.

So far we have talked of story as personal expression and communication, as imaginative creation and recreation of human concerns, as a way of coming to understand the world, and as sympathetic exploration of the lives of others. There is one more aspect that must be given particular emphasis: story as personal, family and community history. This is an area that has become controversial recently, because of the debate over history as a discipline in the National Curriculum. The tension between history as a reflection of national identity and history as the study of differing versions of the past is perhaps a permanent one, just as there is always a tension between the perspective of the individual and that of the group, and between the perspectives of groups and that of the nation-state as a whole. The tension might be thought of as quite a useful one, as long as no one side becomes very much more powerful than any other. Unfortunately, at times of national insecurity, there is a tendency for governments to want more urgently to influence the telling of the nation's story in ways that are conducive to the success of policies. The reforms initiated by the Education Reform Act 1988 (DES 1988) in an attempt to make England and Wales more commercially viable have brought the balance down very strongly on one side – that of the traditional conservative version of Britain's history. The cultural implications of the National Curriculum's Programmes of Study for history, and of the brief outline in the Desirable Outcomes (SCAA 1996), need to be thought through by early years practitioners, for they do not set out to specifically include the history, culture and aspirations of many families and communities. The history of groups who are ethnically different from the white English-speaking majority is not a requirement, nor is that of working-class communities, nor that of women as a social group; nor is the story of the battle for Welsh, Scots and Irish independence a requirement. Yet it is these histories which will be the cultural nourishment of the growing mind, and which will provide the tools with which to understand the world. It is possible to see, in this dilemma, why it is that Zipes (1995) regards storytellers as the most subversive of all agents since, in giving people the idea that they can tell their own stories, they give them the chance to construct and communicate an alternative version of events.

In a democracy, of course, it should be possible to tolerate tensions of this kind. Indeed, it might be said that democracies can only survive to the extent that such differences of perspective *can* be tolerated. This gives the work of the early childhood educator a particular urgency, for children's own stories and their family and community stories must be told while they learn the history of the nation as a whole. From our earlier discussion, the reader will see how the child's self-respect is rooted in and nourished by such stories.

In this discussion we are focusing on the tension between personal and national histories, but in the early years of education there is a similar overall tension as well, between requirements for formal learning and the individual starting points, cultures and rates of progress of individual children. To provide a curriculum which takes account of this tension and finds ways to release it takes more than good intentions, and a curriculum that can incorporate both aims will be a complex and sophisticated one.

The early years practitioners involved in the 'Quality in Diversity' project (Early Childhood Education Forum (ECEF) 1997) worked on one such approach (see Chapter 3 for details. (References to this document are to the draft available at the time of going to press.)) It illustrates both a useful way of proceeding and some of the features of such a curriculum. Within the structure of their 'framework for early learning', the progress of individual children, their own experiences and their own stories can be traced.

We can see an example of this in the work of a childminder who decided to take her group of children to the park specifically because she knew that one child, aged 2 years 3 months, had been there at the weekend with her father and had been playing on some large logs. She hoped that this might help the child to feel more confident within the group and encourage her to talk about the experience with the minder and with the other children. The little girl would have had some interesting experiences which might stimulate her to try to find ways to express herself. She would be able to use the words she already knew, and perhaps learn some new ones that she needed.

In an informal way, the example shows how an approach similar to Quality in Diversity, while giving high priority to children's personal development and perspectives, can also support planning for children to learn what is needed for full participation in the world, now and in later life. It is based on an understanding of how children develop, and is realistic about what can be expected of them. It incorporates an understanding of how attitudes form. It gives the highest priority to children's own self-esteem and self-respect, to their respect for others, and to their enjoyment of and respect for learning.

Something to think further about

How far do the children's own stories and histories feature in the daily and longer-term curriculum plans of your group?

3

An *adaptable curriculum for a changing world*

Play encourages social contact, zest for knowledge, perseverance and self-challenge

Present trends in early education have been characterized in earlier pages as derived from a policy of making education more formal, along the lines of secondary education. This policy has been shown (Blenkin and Kelly 1994) to be unsuitable for young children. It is also unsuitable for the future that children will grow up into. The world is constantly changing, and our ideas about it necessarily have to change as well. There are no certainties, scientific or otherwise; indeed, science itself is constantly changing its interpretation of what we observe about the world. Neither a formal view of learning nor a rigid view of what knowledge is useful can be appropriate to today's world, and even less so to tomorrow's. A Hebrew proverb shows why: 'Do not confine your children to your own learning, for they were born in another time.'

Formal approaches, similar to those of previous generations, are not the way to meet the demands of today's and tomorrow's worlds. Marshall (1997: 36–7) calls for a new approach to education and training:

Revolutionary new insights about the natural world and the human brain are now enabling us to transform the current structures and processes of schooling, and develop learning communities that truly empower the learner and engage the fullness of her capacities.

Why is transformation necessary? I believe unintentionally we have created schools where many children and adults have become intellectually, creatively and emotionally anorexic.

Although her work is based in secondary education and she herself feels that her conclusions do not apply equally to primary education, in fact her work is very much in accord with the early years curriculum and its great potential for adaptability to new ideas, and to the immense range of achievement, learning strategies and special needs of young children.

This quality of adaptability is the most hopeful feature of all for the future. Our fast-changing world requires exactly this openness about new learning and the precise kinds of qualities that characterize early childhood: clear vision, practicality, inventiveness, creativity and sensitivity to one's own and others' feelings. These can hardly be fostered through a curriculum in which the 'right' answer is predetermined and in which children's existing knowledge is ignored in favour of material which they are expected to learn. However, these qualities *can* be promoted through a curriculum which respects children's own perspectives and interests, and rests securely on children's own powerful motivation to learn and their commitment of endless energy and questioning. As young children are driven by their own need to know more, to explore, to question, to think, to imagine, to create, to express and to communicate, they are the ideal learners for those who are prepared to teach informally and flexibly. This kind of curriculum is often described as a 'developmental curriculum' (Blenkin and Kelly 1996: 38) or a 'developmentally appropriate curriculum' (Bredekamp 1987: 3).

The developmentally appropriate curriculum (DAC) is based on a theory of teaching and learning which has at its centre the conviction that education should be shaped in accord with the learners' stage of development, and the knowledge and interests which have emanated from their experiences within the home and community. The strength of this approach to education is that it serves both the need for high-quality subject understanding, knowledge and skills, and the need for children to develop positive attitudes and behaviour as social beings and as learners.

The DAC is not only concerned with subject content. It plans for children to learn in ways which challenge and advance every important aspect – their physical, emotional, social, moral/spiritual, aesthetic/creative *and* cognitive development.

Children learn mainly through their communications with others; through investigating and testing out ideas; through exploration and imagination; through creative representation of their thinking and feeling in imaginative and symbolic activities, in dance, movement, music, drawing, painting, modelling and many other creative forms. When these activities are freely encouraged and supported by the adult, and when they are self-initiated and self-directed, they constitute *play* for the child. Learning through play is recognized and subscribed to as an essential component of developmentally appropriate practice. The following observation is an example of this:

> In an inner-city playgroup the children included three recently-arrived Nigerian children aged 2–3 who spoke little or no English. In fact, they seemed not to feel like speaking to anyone in any language. They communicated with each other exclusively, and only through gesture. The first gestures were invitations to play; one child would hide behind a door, then pop her or his head out, catch the eye of another, then withdraw. Soon, they were following each other in and out of the door from the hall into another room.

Children learn through play, using whatever resources are suitable and to hand. This play was not time-wasting; the children were establishing relationships, and their play deserved to be taken seriously. The staff of the playgroup were able to offer developmentally different kinds of play to satisfy the needs of both these young children and the older ones. The younger children had the freedom to relate to each other through play, because the playgroup followed a DAC.

The freedom to pursue a broad range of play activities is valuable because it encourages social contact, zest for knowledge, perseverance and self-challenge. Moreover, this approach contributes to children's emotional well-being – an aspect which is often overlooked – and enables practitioners to provide for children's individual needs.

Adults who operate a DAC, therefore, base their programmes both on their appropriateness for the age span within the group, and on the extent to which they can be responsive to the individual needs, interests, differences and developmental levels of the children in their charge. This means that they rely very much on the observations and records of the children which they make, to guide them in their curriculum planning. Here adults also try to achieve their educational aims largely by providing 'real' materials, objects, activities and experiences which have interest for, and relevance to, the lives of the children concerned.

This is a kind of curriculum that has to be monitored on a continuous basis, and its quality depends on its in-built ongoing evaluation of what is done, through observation of children and reflection on what has been learned. Observation-based evaluation can produce a curriculum which is capable of providing for attention to individual children's learning, in both the content of learning and in the attitudes and dispositions that are even more important. Because the curriculum is informal, it is easier for practitioners to pay attention to children's individual needs and strengths. This is important for all children, and particularly so for those with special learning needs or disabilities. Parents and practitioners alike see social and emotional development, moral and spiritual education as preparation for participation in a democratic society, and therefore just as valuable as other kinds of learning. The early years of education are a stage when children are highly sensitive to adults' wishes for them, and are very quick to learn from what they see and experience. Children learn more from adults acting as models than if they expressly demand what they want. Formal approaches to the curriculum place more importance on children being able to perform in certain ways than on their development of understanding in their own terms. Yet how else can social skills, emotional development, moral understanding, spiritual growth and education for democracy take place? These are not school subjects to be timetabled, but ways of feeling and acting which have to be learned through daily experience. A pedagogy which is based both on sound principles of child development and on subject knowledge is essential for this learning.

The early years curriculum is perhaps the foremost example of a DAC, in that everything that practitioners do has to be justified according to children's present experience, stages of development and levels of understanding.

Furthermore, the informal approach which is needed only works when it is based on a pedagogy of this sort. It encourages children's strongest motivations to learn in order to promote intellectual development alongside social, emotional, moral, spiritual and democratic development. An informal approach based on the DAC also provides for children's needs to develop their physical capacities and to learn through movement – an essential for health in young children. The many cases in which children under 6 are not able to have continuous access to physical activity and spontaneous play in outdoor learning environments are putting at risk their present and future health.

A curriculum which aims to educate in all these different aspects needs to be built on children's interests, their social relationships, preferred ways of learning and their achievements with their families. This involves giving priority to the major learning processes of active and self-chosen movement, communication, play and self-expression. Children use these processes throughout early childhood, and through them they learn how to understand, share, learn and collaborate with other people; how to use imagination and fantasy; to explore and experiment in safety; and to be creative and to represent their ideas. These learning processes are so interesting and enjoyable to children that they will commit literally hours of effort to making what they do as good as possible. Toddlers practise walking up steps to a low slide with the same determination that can be seen in 4-year-olds learning to walk up a steeply inclined plank; babies teach themselves to walk by trying over and over again and learning from their falls, just as 6-year-olds set themselves to learn new balancing routines.

When these learning processes are linked to the natural activities of childhood, they can give impetus and excitement to learning. They should be given high priority in the allocation of accommodation, time, resources and adult attention. However, the current emphasis on school subjects has made many practitioners, even those working with the under-3s, fearful of giving priority to anything else. An examination of what is involved in supporting children's natural activities in the years before 6 may help to convince readers that in fact subjects are all incorporated in these activities.

In *getting to know the people closest to them* children experience the excitement of discovering how others experience their lives, their personalities and histories. As discussed in Chapter 2, the gripping oral narratives they hear, the stories they read in picture books and their own stories are the foundation of their later interest in literature, history, geography and the arts. A group of 6-year-olds used an atlas in the travel agent's office which was set up in their classroom. Soon they were talking of journeys they had made with their families and pointing to where they thought their holiday destinations were. Suddenly, one child began talking of giants walking across countries and through the sea, using his fingers to show the length of the strides. Later, three of the children drew some maps with representations of the giants' journeys, showing the sea and different countries.

In *investigating the world around them*, children have their first experiences of the natural world with all its beauty and its mysteries. In handling natural materials such as wooden objects or shells, babies begin to come to grips with learning through the five senses. In handling living plants and small creatures, children learn about how other life forms should be cared for (Hurst 1997). Later experiments with water, sand, clay and earth give opportunities for laying the groundwork for understanding science and the value of scientific method. This is later an essential part of learning history as well. One nursery class worked with their teacher on a theme of 'underground', which brought together natural and human activity below the surface, and involved a museum visit and objects buried in the sand tray. The excavation of the foundations of the premises officer's house added another dimension.

Searching for information and asking questions, both of other people and through consulting books, databases and other sources of information, is a skill that is essential for all learning, and is identified in the National Curriculum. In pursuing their interests and concerns, children acquire skills and knowledge about how to find answers to their questions that apply to all kinds of information. A patch of ground outside the nursery doors had been planted by the children with sunflower seeds for a 'race' to see which would be the tallest. It was now autumn and the winner had long been decided, but the big seed heads were still there, visible from inside the room. A group of goldfinches appeared and began to feast on the seeds; Priesh, aged 3, noticed them and was upset that the birds were 'taking the children's flowers'. The nursery worker brought in a booklet about feeding birds and showed Priesh the pictures of birds and the different kinds of food they liked. During the following week she brought in some mixed birdseed for the children to see, and showed them how to match each kind to the picture. One of the parents lent a book about birds, and said how much her children liked going to the park and seeing the ducks. The nursery organized a visit for Priesh and other children, and found when they arrived that there was an information board with pictures of the ducks to help identify them. Because the children enjoyed matching ducks to pictures, the nursery staff planned, when they had the time, to take the children to a local museum where they could see an exhibition about birds. In the meantime, a display of reference books and pictures was arranged near the best place for watching the sunflower heads. Unfortunately, the goldfinches did not return, but the nursery helped children to feed other birds instead. One of the parents showed them how to prepare and eat some of the sunflower seeds themselves.

Thinking is, of course, a complex process with many different forms, and it differs between individual people. Some children are more given to talking, some to drawing, some to physical expression, some to music. Most individuals have their preferred way to do it, but the act of reflecting on what has been experienced is the common element. The reflection is powered by imagination, and is a creative and self-expressive process where the results are tested out against the reality of the world and the people around. Philosophical and logical operations come from this, and can be seen most clearly when children ask questions or make statements that show they are really puzzling about the world. Babies show their delight in exploiting the action of gravity on objects by dropping things; children of 1 and 2 often throw things to see how far they can be made to go; 3- and 4-year-olds may ask about what they have observed happening and show what they have hypothesized already. Navarra (1955) reports on the way his son puzzled over the quicker disappearance of snow from the sunny side of the house, and his search for the explanation of this phenomenon.

How a developmental curriculum can support early learning

1 The practitioners

The quality of the practitioner, and the understanding, knowledge, skill, expertise and commitment that she or he brings, determines the quality of a developmental curriculum.

Understanding: strong traditions of a child development basis for the training of early years practitioners have ensured in the past that practitioners were fitted for their role in supporting children's learning. It is vital that a focus on how children grow and learn is restored to such courses so that newly qualified practitioners, teachers in particular, are able to engage children's minds, feelings and bodies in their learning.

Knowledge and skills: the study of the early years curriculum has been displaced by the introduction of the National Curriculum and the Desirable Outcomes for Children's Learning, which give the impression that the learning of children under 6 is merely the beginning of subject learning, whereas we have shown that it involves much more. The curriculum for children up to the age of 6, *at least*, has to be reinstated as a developmental and specifically early years curriculum. The rest of this chapter will describe this curriculum and the skills which practitioners need in order to provide it for children.

2 The early years curriculum itself

The characteristics of the early years curriculum derive from the fact that most versions of it are built on principles of one kind or another. Gillian Pugh has described (ECEF 1997) how the Quality in Diversity project, which was referred to in Chapter 2, started from the underpinning principles that members of the Early Childhood Education Forum adhered to. The principles were broadly concerned with four interconnected areas:

- the ways in which young children learn: e.g. 'Young children learn best through play, firsthand experience and talk';
- equal opportunities for children to realize their potential: e.g. 'cultural and physical diversity should be respected and valued';
- democratic approaches to education: e.g. 'a proactive anti-bias approach should be adopted and stereotypes challenged';
- the education and training of practitioners: e.g. 'carers and educators should work in partnership with parents' (ECEF 1997: 9).

This basis of principle means that the early years curriculum has clear, broad guidance to offer on issues which are concerned with children's development (how to meet the different needs of individuals within one curriculum framework); with aiming for equality in an unequal world (how to give individuals similar chances when their different cultures, languages, religions and racial identities are not viewed as equally valuable in society); and with examining the political beliefs that permeate different approaches to education (the democratic or anti-democratic aims that underpin policies). This gives the curriculum a conceptual and ethical strength which is of great help in decision-making, where conflicting claims and assertions often conceal the important issues – such as in allocating the most valuable and scarce resource of all, the practitioner's time and attention. For instance, how might the teacher of a Year 1 class decide between hearing each child read every week and taking time to resource, organize and take a part in a classroom 'office' where children are reading, writing and using mathematical skills in play? The participants in the Quality in Diversity project (ECEF 1997) have worked out a system which translates principles into more specific aims, and gives practitioners a way to think through these dilemmas.

The Quality in Diversity project

After many years of working separately, the major providers of care and education services for children under the age of 8 came together in 1994 under the umbrella of the Early Childhood Education Forum to establish an agreed way of approaching the curriculum in care and education settings for young children. The project aimed to develop understanding of how best to meet children's learning needs in the early years of education; to seek a common view of what is an appropriate curriculum for young children; to involve practitioners from the statutory, voluntary and independent sectors in developing this view; to create a continuum of learning for all children from birth to 8; and to improve practice in providing equality of opportunity for all children. The age phases concerned were those from 0 to 3, 3 to 5 and 5 to 8.

Participants believed that all provision of education and care for children under 8 should be developmentally appropriate – it should be planned and provided according to individual children's needs for learning and development. They hoped to spread understanding of the developmentally appropriate curriculum for education in the early years: not to write a syllabus to be followed, but to encourage adults to reflect on how we can all work towards improving our planning and our practice by taking children's emotional, social, physical, communicative and intellectual needs more seriously.

The participants began with 'Foundations of early learning' which all could agree on.

The five foundation statements

Belonging and connecting: from birth, young children are learning to form respectful relationships with adults and other children in families, communities and group settings. They are learning to make choices about their identities as girls and boys and as members of their ethnic/racial, linguistic, social, cultural (and religious) groups.

Being and becoming: from birth, young children are learning self-respect, and feelings of self-worth and identity. They are learning to take care of themselves, and to keep safe and well.

Contributing and participating: from birth, young children are learning to contribute and participate in families and other groups. They are learning to support each other, to care for each other, and to collaborate. They are learning to make choices and to understand how their choices affect others.

Being active and expressing: from birth, young children are mentally and physically active. They are learning to express their ideas, thoughts and feelings, alone and with others, in a variety of ways.

Thinking, imagining and understanding: from birth, young children
begin to think in a variety of ways: wondering, imagining, puzzling,
dreaming, asking questions. They are learning to understand themselves and the world around them. They are learning to think critically
and in a balanced way.

(ECEF 1997: 16)

These statements form the basis of more detailed goals which can be
used to guide and evaluate the provision that is made for children's learning. For instance:

- being and becoming a communicator of increasing skill and confidence (verbal and non-verbal, gestures, signs, dialects and languages);
- being and becoming more aware of written languages and aspects
  of literacy (stories and images, including those on a computer
  screen).

(ECEF 1997: 18)

These goals do not give direct prescriptions of how choices should be
made, but they help practitioners to think through the decisions that have
to be made. If 'being and becoming more aware of written languages and
aspects of literacy' is a goal for children's learning, then a proper valuation
can be put on the classroom 'office' and what the children do there.

This does not mean, however, that each decision has to be thought out
each time from first principles. There are well-established traditions in
early childhood which practitioners can draw on – for instance, the concept of the planned learning environment and of resource-based provision
for learning, such as books, art materials, puzzles, games, sand, water,
clay, bricks, outdoor equipment, etc. The knowledge, understanding and
skill which children need to acquire are learned through these areas of the
planned learning environment and are the essence of the daily curriculum.

Planning

Planning takes place at different levels, but at each level we need to be
aware of how we are providing for children to learn in developmentally
appropriate ways, including imaginative and symbolic play.

Planning long-term

Many practitioners work in settings where there are curriculum requirements such as the National Curriculum or the Desirable Outcomes which

determine what is suitable content in general terms. However, the practitioner has the responsibility for shaping an appropriate implementation of these requirements, and for deciding which require or offer opportunities for developmentally appropriate provision which need interpretation, or are likely to undermine young children's learning. Real-life experiences like gardening, for instance, can form the basis of a practical approach to the curriculum which can include many appropriate ways of learning the uses of literacy, mathematical thinking and technology and science. The conversion of a neglected outdoor play space into an outdoor learning environment inspired a group of 6-year-olds to research the possible developments, to list their preferred options, to measure the space each needed against the space available and to work out ways in which they could garden and watch others gardening without treading on the soil and bringing mud into the classroom.

Planning medium-term

The planned focuses of a period like a few weeks can give opportunities for learning through themes linking the local shops, supermarket or market with provision for imaginative play and role-play. This could link with cooking for the group of children, with outdoor learning and also with the different kinds of food that parents are able to prepare in the setting. Opportunities for reading and writing, for mathematics, for science and technology are there, as well as for history and geography.

Planning short-term

Each day's plans can incorporate children's interests and experiences. For example, an interest in how things change if you water them or add yeast to them can lead to new activities for the next day; this interest can also be the inspiration for a new focus on growth, which could be part of the long-term planning for the future.

The DAC in one child's experience

The experiences of an individual child within a developmental curriculum are illustrated by the following 'learning snapshot' of a child of 4 years 6 months, derived from the records of her nursery teacher and from conversations with her parents.

Rebecca is a leader; she is articulate and imaginative, and other children readily follow her lead in play. Like any good leader, however, she knows that others also have good ideas, and she knows how to take on board their contributions and share the initiative. She is a reader and storyteller with a growing interest in how words are written, and she has already inherited the tradition of fairy-tales and made it her own with stories of kings, queens and castles. She can retell her favourite stories, using the illustrations and her memory to recreate what the text says when it is read. She directs other children in reading her favourite stories, and corrects them when they make a mistake. Her own stories are structured like the stories she has heard, with a beginning, a middle and an end. Her sentences have a sound grammatical structure. She has a strongly logical mind and her later mathematical work will be well-grounded; her teacher has a photograph of her sorting, ordering and ranking the farmyard animals, so that a complete analytical system is revealed, with the different species grouped separately, ranked within the species groups in order of their size. She has been developing her representation of the human figure in drawings and paintings; six months ago her figures were strikingly long with small heads, but now their proportions are more realistic. She is a technologist; she works endlessly to master the cutting and manipulation of tiny pieces of paper, she makes her own finger puppets with which to tell her own stories, and her Duplo castles are planned with a bridge for entry and a space for access to the inside. She uses interactive information technology software, reading the text and commenting on the two different spellings, 'to' and 'too', and asking about their meanings. She recognizes the letters in other children's names on the screen and in the classroom. She is challenging herself physically in learning to use the large outdoor climbing equipment; coming down is the bit she finds most difficult. She is confident and pleasant with adults; she was most hospitable and friendly with a visitor to the class, inviting her to return after dinner and spend more time with her during the afternoon, 'because I stay for dinner now'.

This portrait of Rebecca shows how her first experience of education in a group setting has been one which enabled her to build on her strengths across the board.

To provide learning opportunities that will suit the needs and interests of individuals is demanding, and the practitioner who works to a DAC has to support the standards of her or his work by continuous evaluation.

Evaluating change and professional development

The early years curriculum, in placing such high priority on being flexible and responsive through evaluation of what has been observed, has a capacity for change built into it. This is its chief strength, since it enables practitioners to improve their work continuously and does not impose barriers to the new understandings that come from these changes.

Practitioners who can work like this, learning from what they observe about the children and applying these insights to their own development of understanding, are responsible professionals and more autonomous than others. In the final chapter we discuss practitioner research and professional development, which has been a very fruitful area in the early years. This is because practitioners who successfully follow a DAC are effectively engaged in an enquiring and reflective stance all the time, and in consequence, adapt easily to innovatory methods of improving practice.

Something to think further about

How might the available indoor and outdoor space be organized and resourced to cater for working within a DAC?

4

Play and learning

Play is a powerful force in learning

Certain ground rules emerge clearly from our discussion of the whole concept of the DAC. The essence of these is that teaching is most effective
when it provides opportunities for learning in ways that motivate and
challenge children to draw on everything they know and can do, so as to
take their learning and development further. In this way, practitioners can
meet the all-round needs of children, whatever their present achievements, their abilities and/or their linguistic and cultural backgrounds may
be. As a result, apart from children becoming successful lifelong learners,
and acquiring attitudes, knowledge and skills which will serve them well
in future endeavours, this approach is most likely to produce adaptable,
imaginative, creative and highly motivated people.

Does society want people like this? Do we want people with open
minds, who can learn from others whoever they are, and from new
developments both locally and globally? It is important to examine this
question carefully, because if we support the DAC, we must recognize that
creative and imaginative people are likely to be the result. If that is not
what we believe is good for society, we must abandon the notion of the
DAC at once. Why is it important to have creative and imaginative and
questioning members of society? It seems self-evident that in order to
generate new ideas and move forward, society must have such people.
Clearly, the arts of writing, painting, sculpture, architecture, dance, music
and so forth need boldness and courage and imagination to try things out
in order to represent thoughts and feelings, and to communicate them to
others. Imagination, too, underlies feelings of sympathy, empathy, and
concern for other people – qualities which are sorely needed in our world
in which people are still fighting each other, somewhere or other in almost
every continent.

Moving away from the arts for the moment to other areas of knowledge,
think back, say, to Archimedes in his bath. It was because of his questioning mind that he asked himself about the rise and fall of the water when
he got in and out of the tub – and think of the fundamental change in
human understanding, through the centuries, that has followed as a result.
Scientists and mathematicians like Einstein, Bertrand Russell, Marie Curie
and Stephen Hawking all used their questioning and imaginative minds
to pose fundamental questions, and through 'lateral' thinking, seek
answers to them. We do not of course suggest that we want or could have
masses of geniuses like these, but we do aim to encourage people who will
be creative in their own domains, and be receptive to the new thinking,
creativity and discoveries of the utterly brilliant few. We live now in a com-
petitive, technological world, based on economic interests, with power
resting in the hands of a few who are not, by and large, concerned about
their responsibility to those whose fate depends on their decisions. As we

said in Chapter 3, we do not know what knowledge and skills the children of today will need in the future, fast-changing world, and the way in which forthcoming generations will be able to maintain their place in it with some success will depend on the extent to which, as a people, we can be innovative and use our creative intelligence.

In the adult world of work, we need creative and adaptable approaches. A conformist, traditional view has been that middle and upper management should maintain a distance between itself and the rest of the workforce. There may be many reasons for this – class divisions, or fear of loss of power or of rebellious workers. Whatever the case, divisions between 'bosses' and workers mean that any creative or imaginative ideas which workers may have had, have largely been denied expression, to the detriment of all concerned.

In recent years, Japanese entrepreneurs have come to recognize the greater strength their entire business gains when they draw on, and involve the ideas and vision of, the workers, who are, after all, fundamental to the success of the whole enterprise.

Perhaps even more important than the management versus worker issue is the question of the ways in which repetitive and mechanical work, in factories for example, affect the creativity of those who unhappily find themselves tied to such tasks. We have to ask how it is that top management is itself unimaginative enough to plan for and allow such mindless occupations to take place at all. What has happened in *their* personal development which has dulled their imagination in such a way that they seem unable to put themselves in the position of their workers? Again, how is it possible that the workers can bear to undertake such work? Economic factors aside, has *their* imagination been so underdeveloped that they can tolerate carrying out mindless activities day after day? Have they lost their inventiveness through lack of encouragement to develop and exploit it? Or is it, as Erich Fromm suggests, that in the attempt to escape from the feelings of insignificance which the power of others has brought about,

> the individual ceases to be himself. He adopts entirely the kind of personality offered to him by cultural patterns; and he therefore becomes exactly as all others are, and as they expect him to be . . . The person who gives up his individual self and becomes an automaton, identical with millions of other automatons around him, need not feel alone and anxious. *But the price he pays, however, is high; it is the loss of his self.*
>
> (Fromm 1966:160, emphasis added)

What does it take to bring about a change in management attitude which will lead to profound alterations in the ways in which an institution

is organized? Again, Japanese entrepreneurs have shown the huge benefits of involving the workforce not only in decision–making, but in working at a variety of tasks and in a variety of ways. In car manufacture, for
example, instead of a worker carrying out a single task continuously, and
as a separate individual, he now works in a team on building a car as a
whole. In this way workers' interest is obviously increased; they have the
rewarding experience of shared teamwork; and they also gain considerable satisfaction from being part of creating a whole, clearly visible object.

These examples have been to do with the adult world – the 'end prod-
ucts', if you like, of a long process begun in childhood. It was important to
consider them, because the ways in which adults behave in society have
much to do with what has happened to them in early childhood. So we
return now to children, and consider how these qualities of imagination
and creativity, together with a zest for knowledge and the understanding
of how to acquire it, can be fostered or inhibited.

In Chapter 3 we outlined what we mean by the DAC, as well as discussing the main ways in which young children learn. We emphasized the
important role which play has in learning, and the fact that it is one of the
essential components of a DAC. We now wish to explore this in more
depth.

It is notoriously difficult to try to define what one means by 'play', and
it may well be that this is a major reason for its being so widely misunderstood as a merely frivolous, recreational activity. This is, indeed, what
most adult play is about. We play golf, or tennis, or go swimming after
a hard day's work. We escape from the hardships of everyday life by
'playing' the horses, or practising our flower–arranging, or completing
our watercolour painting. In other words play, for adults, is indeed recreational, often light-hearted, and certainly not part of the 'serious business
of life'. But for children, play has a very different meaning, purpose and
significance, and we adults have to 'take it seriously'.

In trying to pin down the nature of play, researchers and theorists down
the ages have highlighted the fact that whatever it is, play embraces a great
deal of children's activities and behaviour, and has different purposes for
them at different stages in their development. So we have exploratory play
(Hutt 1966), which is a precursor to problem-solving skills; practice play
(Piaget 1962), in which constant repetition of actions helps in mastering
them; sociodramatic play (Garvey 1977; Smilansky 1980), where social
interactions have at their core the creation and sharing of rules in imagi-
natively created situations; symbolic play (Piaget 1962; Vygotsky 1962;
Bruner et al. 1976), which includes imaginative and creative play, and in
which children pretend that they and/or objects are transformed into
something or someone else. This last type of play is of such significance in

children's development that we will return to it again. Suffice it to say at this point that these are simply descriptions of types of play, and still do not deal with what it is.

The best way forward, perhaps, is to adopt an approach which does not take an either/or explanation, but encompasses several interpretations. This has in fact been suggested by Pellegrini (1991) who, in drawing together various threads from theories, shows how we can define play within three dimensions – play as disposition, as context, and as observable behaviour.

'Play as disposition' is to do with children's need to explore; with their intrinsic motivation; with the ways in which they pay attention; with their active engagement and involvement with the world around them. These dispositions are intrinsic to learning, and to children becoming lifetime learners. Their development is also very much dependent on the emotional well-being of the child, which acts as a springboard for confident exploration and experiment (Bowlby 1969; Laevers 1991).

'Play as context' involves the notion of spontaneity, together with a lack of any predetermined end in view, and the freedom to choose, initiate, direct and control pursuits oneself.

'Play as observable behaviour' derives from the different stages of play which evolve during early childhood, and which have been identified, in particular, by Piaget (1962) and Bruner (1974). These include the development from sensorimotor to symbolic play and games with rules.

When we are able to observe a combination of these three dimensions in children's activities, we can safely say that we are seeing play.

Whilst this 'definition', like most others, has its limitations, it gives us a clearer and broader base from which to make decisions about why and how to include play in our educational provision. It also helps to justify the seemingly vague but widely acknowledged view that 'I may not know what play is, but I recognize it when I see it!'

Activities undertaken in this way truly involve the child, and so are powerful ways of learning. This learning is not only to do with the acquisition of knowledge and skills, but embraces coming to understand the needs and claims of others; acquiring physical prowess; learning the art of communication through language and the arts; and, very importantly, learning about oneself, both as an individual and in relation to others. To 'know thyself' has a great deal to do with a person's inner strength and happiness.

If we agree that education is principally about promoting the inner resources of children, so that they are soon able to stand on their own two feet and make their way in the world with integrity and courage, we must ensure that we plan for and encourage play throughout the early years.

Unhappily, and especially during the last few years when the pressures and demands of the National Curriculum have borne down on teachers and other early years practitioners, the spontaneity intrinsic to true play is too often eliminated in schools. This has come about because of the emphasis placed on attaining particular skills and certain information. It is as though the designers of the NC suffered from the delusion that by accumulating a great number of facts we will end up with an understanding of reality.

Our plea, therefore, is that the curriculum in playgroups, private nurseries, home settings, nursery schools and classes, and especially in reception and Year 1 classes, should be designed to incorporate a great deal of play, in terms of both the resources on offer and the understanding and intentions of the practitioners. This is not to say that it should be a substitute for the more structured, direct guidance and instruction which is also appropriate in educational settings such as a school; what is needed is a balance between the two approaches.

This is an example of what we mean. The following two incidents took place in the same reception classroom, on the same morning, with the same child, Julie, aged 4 years 4 months.

Sitting at a table with seven other 4-year-olds, Julie had spent 12 minutes completing the task given to her of matching the correct number of Unifix® bricks with the pictures of them on pre-prepared cards. The numbers ranged from 1 to 5 depending on which card was given her. She completed about four cards, waiting patiently between each for the teacher to check that they were correct, before moving on to the next one.

Julie was finally released from this 'work', and went over to a partitioned-off corner of the room where a 'kitchen corner' had been created, with a large plastic kitchen unit, plates and cups and saucers etc. She turned to the observer and said, 'I love kitchens like this,' and immediately started investigating what was on offer. She was soon joined by another girl, Lucy. Julie said, 'I'm the Dad, and you can be the Mum. Put the toast in here' [the toaster]. Julie started to set the table for two, when a third child, Cheryl, joined them.

Julie: Do you want to be the cat? Or do you want to be the sister? I'm the Dad and she's the Mum.

Cheryl opted for being the cat, and got down on her hands and knees, and crawled over to the plate of 'milk' which Julie put down for her. Julie then continued setting the table, now for three. She placed three side-plates correctly, three cups on three saucers; three sets of knives and forks; and put three 'sausages' into three 'rolls' onto each plate. She turned round to see the 'cat' looking inside the oven, and said, 'Cats do not do that,' and shut the oven. At this point, after just ten minutes, the teacher announced that it was time to tidy up, and the play came to an end.

It was interesting to observe how much higher Julie's level of involvement was when she was in the 'kitchen', compared with the work with the Unifix® bricks, and how animated she became whilst counting out and matching the cups and saucers etc. In this self-chosen activity, she showed clearly that she was highly skilled in 'matching', and had a good concept of what it meant. And yet she had struggled, rather anxiously, with the earlier task of matching the Unifix® bricks to the pictures on the cards. This is also a good example of what we mean by play – a self-chosen activity, with intrinsic motivation high, the freedom to follow the pursuit as wished, and the opportunity to practise and/or reinforce what the child knows. Moreover, there was a good deal of symbolic and imaginative play, which started almost from the very moment Julie went into the kitchen.

If this teacher had used play as her starting point, and had organized the activities in the classroom so that the children could choose from a variety of play experiences to do with different 'subjects', she would not only have been able to meet the needs and interests of the children more satisfactorily, but would also have made her own task of stimulating learning a much easier one. Marie Guha's (1996: 2) 'economic' argument for play in school, and especially in reception classes, is appropriate here.

> The economic argument suggests that the management of learning in the classroom is most efficient when play is included and valued in the curriculum. Efficiency is enhanced because teachers have to spend less time trying to motivate children to learn; because teaching is more effective as teachers achieve a better 'fit' between their instruction/explanation and the child's thinking; and because the quality of the child's learning is enhanced when it is in tune with self-directed, voluntary involvement. For these reasons, to use present-day jargon, the inclusion of play is 'cost-effective' . . . Inclusion of play in the curriculum does not mean the substitution of instruction by teacher involvement in children's play. As argued earlier, the efficient management of learning includes both, and requires a better balance between teacher-initiated and child-initiated pursuits in the classroom.

Using play as a starting point implies that the adult is fully aware of its significance for the child's learning and all-round development. It means that the adult recognizes, when planning the curriculum, that he/she must seek a balance between giving the children opportunities to learn through their self-initiated play, and between providing learning which is more formally negotiated between the child and the adult. It also means that the practitioner is at least as much concerned with the processes of learning as with its outcomes.

How children learn should be at the root of our approach to teaching and learning, and we have spelt this out in Chapter 1. The fact that children's play is such a powerful force in their learning means that we must make sure that it is intrinsic to our provision, in whatever setting, throughout the first six or seven years of life.

It is much easier to ensure this when children are of non-statutory school age, i.e. under 5. There is generally more acceptance of the fact that these children learn through their play. Or, at least, this had been the case up until the mid-1980s, when, without any public announcement or genuine consultation, our 4-year-olds were allowed to be incorporated into reception classes. Moreover, when the Nursery Voucher system was introduced in 1996, it became almost the norm that children should enter the reception class at 4, alongside 5-year-olds. It is from these classes that the opportunities for play have largely disappeared. This has a great deal to do with pressures from the National Curriculum, and from parents who are anxious for their children to 'get on'. It also has to do with the fact that so many of these classes have upwards of 35 children with one teacher (or maybe with an assistant for part of the time), who may feel that he/she will have more control over both learning and behaviour if children are taught in more formal ways. Our example above, with Julie, highlights what we mean. Here are some more.

On a visit to a local school, a practitioner observed the following in a reception class of thirty-five 4- and 5-year-olds:

> A pile of finished work lay on a table. The 4-year-old group had been directed to stick pieces of twisted macaroni onto identical outlines of a rabbit, which the teacher had prepared in advance and given to each child. The children then had to paint over the macaroni in brown paint, which the teacher had again prepared in advance.

What was the teacher hoping that the children would learn? Sticking pieces of twisted macaroni onto identical outlines of the rabbit seemed to be related to the rabbit theme which prevailed throughout the school. Was it that the experience of painting over the macaroni in brown paint was intended as an experience of texture, because the surfaces were not flat? Perhaps it was to do with area, because the surfaces had to be covered? Possibly, creative art was intended? If the teacher had organized a workshop area where painting and model-making and cutting and sticking were available, and the children had the freedom and time to experiment and play with them, all of those aims could have been achieved, with the children adding much more through their own imaginative interpretation of the materials.

This can be seen in the next example:

A class of 4-year-olds were making puppets as part of the class follow-up on the story of *The Little Gingerbread Boy*. The nursery nurse had prepared a display on puppetry and puppets, including some shadow, glove and spoon puppets, a simple cloth puppet and a paper puppet, some finger puppets and a marionette. She had asked the children to bring in from home anything that they had which could be used to make puppets. She assembled all the materials on a table, together with paste, scissors, sequins, string, non-pointed sticks, plasticine and so on. The children who chose to come and join in were invited to make their own puppets. Some children had previously made paper-bag puppets, and approached the task with confidence. Others were newcomers to the idea, and needed more help. Diane, a child with special needs, came to the table with her welfare assistant, and took a piece of brightly coloured paper and drew a circle on it. With a little hint from her helper, she added eyes, nose and mouth. This was the most detailed face she had drawn so far. She cut round the face and with help, stuck string on the back. She was now able to 'dance' the puppet up and down, and was delighted with her achievement which, for her, was a considerable one. Compared with some of the others, which were more complex, Diane's puppet was simple and basic. But because it was such an achievement for her, it was an important experience, both in terms of her learning and of the boost to her self-confidence and self-esteem.

Subsequently, the children and the nursery nurse made a simple puppet theatre from a large cardboard box, and Diane joined the other children in giving puppet shows as and when they wished.

Again:

One wet afternoon, in a nursery school, Mrs H was having a rather bad time and complaining about the noise. Matthew, aged 4, drew a picture of 'Mrs H with a headache on her head'. Her head, in the drawing, was surmounted by a heavy black bar running from side to side.

If we compare these examples with that of the rabbits, it is clear that the former could not possibly be called creative, as there was no opportunity for the children to be inventive, spontaneous, or original in any sense of the word. On the other hand, the puppet activities were genuinely creative, challenging the children to pursue their own ideas, and to do their best at their own level. They gave true satisfaction to the children, who learned a great deal through this guided play. As for Matthew – he showed how he was able to build on his imagination, using a new way of seeing, doing and interpreting. It was perhaps also a demonstration of a young child empathizing with someone else. This was truly original thinking.

In another reception class:

> The whole class was to engage in 'doing number', and the 4-year-olds were directed to work with cards, which required matching five objects to the number 5. Some had to make five snakes with plasticine, some had to match five Unifix® squares onto five printed squares, and others had to make a 'fence for the field' with five previously cut-up pieces of drinking straw, and then make five sheep from plasticine to go inside the field. The 5-year-olds were following up a discussion on number, using pre-prepared cards on which different numbers of shapes had to be added to, to complete a required amount: e.g. three triangles had to be added to two, and the total written down. Kylie (4y. 3m.) looked up with a worried expression and said, 'I've made a mistake!' The observer said, 'Oh dear, we all make mistakes sometimes, don't we?' Kylie seemed rather relieved, and her anxiety lessened. When the teacher came over to check the work, Kylie said she had made a mistake. The teacher, without a word, erased the error with an eraser. It was then time to go to the hall, and the cards were packed away. The teacher was not without help that morning – she had two assistants who were engaged in seeing that these tasks were being carried out.

In these examples, the activity was teacher-initiated, and in this sense was imposed on the children. It also gave no recognition to the differences in the levels of understanding which each individual had. Clearly Kylie, anxious about having 'made a mistake', was under considerable strain to try and do correctly what the teacher had required of her. Moreover, the 'mistake' was not discussed with her in order to clarify it, and she was left somewhat in mid-air, and with a feeling of failure. Kylie needed reassurance from her teacher that 'mistakes' are no 'bad thing'; she needed help, through discussion and manipulation of triangular objects, to find out the 'answer'; but most of all, she needed many opportunities to play with numbers of objects, putting them together, taking some away and so on, with the teacher intervening only when help was clearly needed, in order to take the child further in her understanding and thinking. Again we think back to Julie, counting and matching perfectly in her play, and it is reasonable to surmise that if Kylie had had the opportunity for a similar type of activity, she would have shown that she had, in fact, a clear understanding of what three plus two adds up to.

We can also contrast these examples with that given in Chapter 1 (pp. 33–4), where Troy was classifying the different animals according to their visible characteristics. Here was a 4-year-old engaged in an important mathematical activity through his own self-chosen, self-initiated play. The adult's role was to observe what was happening, intervene at an appropriate moment, and with her knowledge of the child himself, help him to take his thinking further.

In Chapters 1 and 3 we have given examples of children, through their play, beginning to acquire concepts in science, maths, language and literature, and to represent and communicate their ideas in a variety of ways. We also highlighted the creative aspects of learning and development, because these are often undervalued, and practitioners in general could do more, through a wider range of resources, to stimulate children to take part in exciting, imaginative and creative experiences.

Partly because of the 'outside' pressures mentioned earlier, the social development of young children can also often be given insufficient attention. If we are concerned with the education of the whole child, we have to consider social and personal development as well as cognitive progress. How best do we help young children to learn to share with others; to accept the needs of others; to be sympathetic towards others and concerned about their welfare; to come to learn about themselves, both as individuals and in relation to other people? The only way in which these qualities can develop and have true meaning is through experience. It is through interacting with others, being confronted by their needs, having to compromise, that children learn to take their place in society in a positive way. If we observe children closely, it becomes obvious that most of this learning is done during their play. It is done when children are truly involved in their chosen activities, and during these early years this is largely when they are playing.

John (3y. 6m.) was trying to wriggle into a chicken costume which he had found in the dressing-up box. He had to get into it from the feet upwards, as it was made like a body suit. He was clearly having difficulty, and James (4y. 3m.) went over to him, and without a word between them he started to help John. He managed to get the stockinged legs on, followed by the rest of the costume, but then had problems himself, when he got to doing up the zip at the back. He struggled and persisted, and finally the teacher, who had been watching, could hold back no longer, and moved across and said, 'Can you manage, James?' She then held the two sides of the material together, and James was able to pull the zip up. Success all round! John ran off flapping his 'wings', and James was satisfied with the help he had given.

It was interesting that there was no verbal exchange between the two children, and yet there seemed to be a tacit understanding that James would be able to help John, as long as he cooperated by remaining still! It was a clear example of one child recognizing another's need, and offering to satisfy it. It is worth noting that the teacher left the children to sort things out for themselves, until she realized that frustration would set in, and moved in to help. She also refrained from doing the zip up for James, but helped him in such a way that he could finally do it himself. This was also a good example of the child-initiated, child-directed, adult-supported play which is an essential component of developmentally appropriate practice.

It is important to emphasize that we do not think that it is *only* through play activities that young children learn. There needs to be the balance, which we mentioned earlier, between children's self-directed play and the practitioner's more formally guiding instruction. If this is achieved, the child can be offered experiences which truly meet his or her needs.

How to get this balance? There are of course many ways, but perhaps at the core of them lies the notion of child and practitioner *sharing intentions* about aims, and ways and means of achieving them. This may sound somewhat over-optimistic, and yet there is plenty of evidence of very young children being capable and willing to negotiate and plan and carry out what is to be done during the day (Hohmann *et al.* 1979). The more this type of discussion and cooperation and agreement is entered into, the more children are happy to take part in all types of learning, and the easier the task is for the practitioner. More than that, the practitioner is more likely and able to recognize, cater for, and monitor individual needs and capabilities. This too lies at the core of a developmentally appropriate curriculum.

Finally, the authors recognize that practitioners will never have enough time to do everything in the way they would like to. However, we believe that adopting a developmentally appropriate approach will mean that they can choose to operate in ways which are more effective for children's personal and learning needs.

Something to think further about

For many practitioners, both time and space are in very short supply. How can the limitations of these restrictions be overcome in order to create play opportunities?

5

Observation: underpinning appropriate education

Good observation helps us to be more expert in how children learn

Previous chapters have emphasized some key points about the early years of education: the necessity of understanding children's development in all areas in order to support individual children's learning: the importance of opportunities for enhancing self-respect and self-discipline that help us all to be good learners (Chapter 2); the need for a curriculum model that takes account of developmental insights which enable practitioners to make educational provision that is appropriately challenging for all children (Chapter 3); and the necessity of providing for children's playful and spontaneous activity in learning in order to exploit their developmentally determined learning power (Chapter 4).

Each of these necessities of good education in the early years rests on the ability of practitioners to understand children's development and to learn from observation how to use their knowledge and understanding to further individual children's learning in an educational setting. This chapter is about how to observe and how to learn from observation. The role of observation is wide; it helps us to make decisions about whom, how, when and where to observe, and it helps us to understand and benefit from what it is that we have discovered after the observations are done. Observation also enables us to evaluate our work and find ways to improve our practice, to extend our expertise and, by self-questioning, to learn more about the education of young children.

Observation should provide the justification for statements about education; it is the source of evidence for education theory which rests upon carefully structured research, some of it using evidence gathered from many children and some of it gathered from in-depth studies of individuals. Both help practitioners to be more expert in how children learn. But the knowledge gained from these studies has to be applied with understanding, and it is the theory of child development which is the source of this understanding. Without applying child development theory, practitioners are highly unlikely to be able to teach effectively. The role of observation is to help practitioners make links between theory and practice, and to see how general rules of development apply to individual children and specific circumstances.

Observation and the links between theory and the real world

All disciplines of knowledge, such as the traditional subjects, the scientific ways of looking at the world, medicine and the arts, embody both theory and practice. The interaction between these two enables us to understand what we currently perceive or experience, and to grow in expertise. Everything we aim to do in education rests on knowledge, yet all knowledge must be kept constantly up to date by being tested and rethought. The test of reality enables us to assess the value of our knowledge, yet at the same time is limited by its very realness. So we continue to need theory. A doctor confronted with a child who is delayed in speaking, draws first on knowledge of theory about the development of speech and then on her or his understanding of the meaning of this knowledge, which has been gained from experience of the ways in which various processes and events have affected children. This understanding influences the development of skills that are needed to help the patient. While this is happening, the doctor is testing existing knowledge and understanding by applying it to the new situation, and will often find unexplained discrepancies or even sheer contradictions between established theory and what is present. These discrepancies cause questions to arise, and the effort to find answers to these questions is invaluable in adding to the doctor's stock of knowledge and understanding about speech delay. This new level of expertise will make the doctor more expert and understanding of the general issues in speech delay, and will also help with the next child who is seen. Some of these questions may draw attention to areas where the doctor's understanding and skill need development, or to assumptions that appear to be wrong, and sometimes to where theory needs to be re-evaluated.

The whole process of learning, understanding and testing knowledge is roughly as in Figure 5.1. In a similar way, knowledge of human development alerts us to what we can hope to learn from observing children, and our understanding grows from relating what we see them do to our existing knowledge. It also matters very much for our own learning and development; even in comparatively simple tasks knowledge becomes out of date if it is not constantly renewed. When we observe and reflect on observations, we have the opportunity to test out the theory to which we adhere in the light of our experience. Many practitioners may not feel in a position to reflect critically on accepted theory and its application without guidance and support, and it is good that there are at least three major research and development projects which do this; these are described in Chapter 7. The value of these projects is not only that they help practitioners to improve their professional expertise and understanding; it is essential for children's equality of opportunity that practitioners should be proficient in observing, in learning from observation and in applying what they learn to their work.

Observation and equal opportunities

Every human being, child and adult, deals with events on the basis of knowledge and understanding about what has happened before. Yet what has happened before does not ever completely repeat itself. This matters

Figure 5.1   Three stages of understanding and expertise

Knowledge from studying existing theory and research

↓

Understanding (and skill based on this) from applying knowledge

↓

Questioning from noting discrepancies, leading to deeper understanding/greater skill in specific situations, and possibly adding to knowledge in general

---

particularly where we have responsibility for others, for if we treat them as if they were the same in every way as those who came before, we may do them an injustice. It is vital for equality of opportunity that we accept our need to observe and reflect before we take decisions, because all of us are predisposed to see children according to our own limited experience and prejudices, and we need a different viewpoint if we are to do justice to children – all children.

Thus, we have to observe individual children in order to identify and apply appropriate kinds of educational provision for them. We need observation to understand children and monitor their progress, particularly since children come from a variety of classes and social backgrounds, with different cultures, languages and religions. They may also have a disability or special gift. Without observation we struggle to give individual girls and boys, with all their differences, a stimulating and meaningful experience of education and a full curriculum.

The central government policies which ruled out child development as an appropriate study for intending teachers in the years following the introduction of the National Curriculum were influenced by a strange misunderstanding. Knowing how humans develop and learn, and how their learning influences their development as well as vice versa, is essential to the effective teaching of any subject matter, skill, attitude or understanding. However, child development was interpreted as being opposed to the successful learning of subjects, and courses in child development were denied accreditation.

This policy undermined the ability of teachers to give children opportunities that match and then build on their existing understanding, for children's learning proceeds by each child's own efforts and experiences. For instance, research based on many studies of children has confirmed that children under the age of 6 are at the stage of building up, defining and refining their concepts of people and objects in the world around them, using the experiences and explanations they have had. Children under 2 often claim cows as a kind of dog at first, whilst older children understand that apples and pears, though different from one another, are both fruit. The long-term continuous study of a young boy referred to in Chapter 3 found that his definition of a garage was that it had a particular kind of opening arrangement; he could not agree that 'garages' with different doors were real garages (Navarra 1955).

The value of this kind of understanding is that practitioners can extend it by analogy to other children. The risk is that, without some knowledge of the actual individual children in question, the patterns of development may be applied mistakenly, under- or over-estimating children because of a lack of knowledge and understanding of how their own development is proceeding. For this reason, assessment of individuals should be based on regular observation to ensure accuracy.

The value of assessments from observation rather than from performance in prearranged tasks can be seen in the conclusions that the teacher of Rebecca (described in Chapter 3) was able to draw from observation over a long period of time. This is how she described her attitudes to learning, beginning with science:

> In terms of science what was most important was how she developed the process skills, how confident she was about what she knew and how willing she was to take risks to develop and broaden that knowledge. She valued opportunities to talk with adults and other children and to research her interests using information books.
>
> A more general observation about her approach to learning would be that the informality [of the setting's programme] allowed her to pursue a particular interest across time as well as across curriculum areas. A whole day or more may have been taken up addressing an interest that came with her from home or that was developed in school, and she had control of her time. She responded well to necessary breaks such as meal times and end of sessions and added her own when she took natural pauses that were in keeping with her flow of thought and interest. Because she was allowed the time to immerse herself she was not frustrated if she had to be required, unexpectedly, to interrupt her work.
>
> For Rebecca, school was just another of her learning environments.

The distinction between performance in formal targets and the kind of learning which leads to lifelong achievement is highlighted in this brief study. Rebecca has had time and opportunity to develop far more than would be required by the 'Desirable Outcomes', yet she is also clearly going to be ready to achieve in the National Curriculum as soon as she starts infant school. In English, mathematics, technology, information technology, physical development, art and religious education she is already a high achiever, yet she has not had to sever the motivating links with her personal interests and imaginative life in the process. It is not only her academic achievement which has been safeguarded; her social and emotional development has been assured as well. Yet without observation this progress could not have been recorded, nor could the curriculum that enhanced her learning have been developed.

Reliable information is needed if a well-matched curriculum is to be provided, and it has to be obtained from observation of the children concerned. The specific purposes for which the information is needed shape the kind of observation we find most helpful.

Observation is involved in much of the work of practitioners: clear information and examples are needed for assessment; for investigation of individual children's learning where there are queries about possible difficulties; for immediate use in planning for individuals and groups; for evaluation and development of plans on a longer-term basis; and for the practitioner's self-development referred to above. The nature, frequency, duration and analysis of observations should be planned to reflect these needs. The criteria for reliability in observations will partly depend on their appropriateness for the task; however, there are certain criteria which should apply to all observations.

Criteria for reliable observation

'Objective' observation is more of a concept than a reality; yet even though all observers are likely to be less than objective, objectivity can be aimed for. What children do and say can be described as precisely as possible without interpretation, so that even someone who was not present can picture what was seen and heard and make a valid judgement on this basis.

Questions can be asked which will help to preserve objectivity. Is the amount of detail obtained of a similar depth, even if the content is very different? For instance, if a child does not engage with an activity where others do, is the non-engagement and the alternative behaviour recorded with the same care? Do continuous observations of individual children for assessment and monitoring of development involve parents? Are children's portfolios of work used as evidence? Baseline assessment must not be allowed to draw attention away from the much greater benefits of the more reliable kinds of assessment that are based on a range of evidence collected at different times when children are in their normal setting and not in a test situation.

Are all the observations that are to be used for a particular purpose structured in the same way? For instance, if a new approach is being monitored, will comparable evidence of learning in all the children be available? It is important to make each observation pull its weight, and regular classroom observation for curriculum planning can contribute to records on individual children.

Interpreting observations

Once the observation has been collected, interpretation can begin. It is helpful to be clear about what is being looked for, if there is a specific aim in mind. However, it is also very enlightening to observe children to find out their interests and concerns, in which case a broad range of evidence will be of interest.

Again, there are criteria for reliable interpretation, whatever the focus of the observation. The first must concern making sure the stages are kept separate – collecting evidence must come before analysing and reflecting on what has been learned. If information from several observations is going to be compared, it is important to compare like with like, and to be aware of ways in which observations may not be directly comparable. It is also important to be sure that one has considered as many possibilities as one can; again, each individual's experiences predispose towards a particular interpretation, and it is helpful to consult others for their views. When we consider the possibility of another person interpreting the evidence differently, the value of making what was observed as objective as possible, and distinguishing fact from interpretation, becomes clear. It may seem hard for practitioners to have to keep all this in mind as well as the subject content of the curriculum, but the benefits are great; in fact, they can make the difference between a powerless and defensive position and a powerful and professional approach.

When practitioners are willing to deepen their knowledge by investigating their own practice and working on ways to improve it, they are self-evaluating. Self-evaluation can find a way through difficult situations, resolve problems, and help practitioners to make their efforts much more successful.

Something to think further about

The teacher in a Year 1 class wishes to enhance his/her children's talking and listening skills. How might the use of observation help to achieve this?

6

Parents and practitioners: sharing education

Children's emotional well-being starts with their relationship with parents

When we consider the relationship between parents and practitioners, the need for a developmental view of the curriculum is clear. In all but a very small proportion of families, parents (and carers who fulfil that role) are the agents who provide the context of each child's first learning. Writers such as Trevarthen (1993) and wide-ranging analyses of many research studies (e.g. the Carnegie Corporation of New York 1994) show the formative role of the parent's engagement with the child. This offers both the stimulus that presents the child with something new to deal with, and also the response which shapes the child's learning from the encounter. To give an example:

> Two babies, Eleanor and Mark, are cousins. Mark is 18 months old and Eleanor is three months. They live quite close to each other and to their grandmother, whose daughter is Eleanor's mother; and whose son is Mark's father. The grandmother is delighted to help the young families by caring for the children when she is free. She finds the babies fascinating in their differences and similarities. One thing that particularly interests her is that she can always calm and reassure Eleanor by singing to her the songs that she sang to her own children when they were little, but she has noticed that, at the same age and now, Mark's response is not the same. He responds to the songs and comfort strategies that his own mother and her mother use, which she herself, his paternal grandmother, has now learned. The babies have learned to be comforted in different ways.

As we have seen, recent research such as that of the Carnegie Corporation (1994) shows that it is not only the particular kinds of initiative and response that parents use with their babies that are important, but rather the levels and suitability of the interaction. The closer the relationship between parent and child, the more likely it is that there is a good match between the communications of each side, and that the child's growing understanding, knowledge and skills are rooted in experience shared with the parents. Emotional well-being, which as we have shown affects learning, is also founded on the relationship between child and parent.

When it comes to educational and care settings outside the home, a new stage begins. There has to be an opening up of this parent and child world to other influences, and the practitioner has to learn something of what has gone on so far in order to help the child make a transition into the world beyond the familiar one.

We have to think what it means for the practitioner that parents are the first in the field with their influence on children's development and learning. We have to ask ourselves what it means for parents that they know the child best but that the practitioner has a responsibility for decisions about the child's learning. We need to reflect on what can happen when to this basic difference of responsibility is added a contrast of culture and experience of life. Working in partnership is not just about the two very different spheres of home and educational setting. It is also about people from different cultures learning to work together for the good of the child.

Human beings live in divided societies. People who appear to be different from the so-called mainstream are often looked down upon by members of the dominant group. Judgements by practitioners about parents as members of particular social groups or about parents as partners in their children's education, are sometimes based on beliefs about particular groups. If parents as individuals belong to groups that are not part of the dominant group in society, stereotyped views of such ethnic minority groups can affect how the parents are perceived and what the expectations are for their children. Decisions have to be made fairly, but also with sympathy.

An African-Caribbean mother and father obtained a part-time place for their daughter Sarah in a nursery school, but they really wanted one of the full-time places that they knew were available. The head explained to them that only in real emergencies, such as illness at home or concern for the child's safety, were children allowed to go straight into a full-time place. These places, which were valued highly because they made it easier for parents to work, were usually offered after the child had spent one or two terms in a part-time place. Sarah's parents were upset because they needed both incomes to support the family, and another child was expected. The interview was rather an uncomfortable one.

Later, Sarah's mother asked if she could leave Sarah until mid-afternoon on the days when she had to go to the clinic at the hospital, as she found it a strain looking after Sarah while she waited and during the examination. The head refused, explaining that while she could do this for one family, she could not do it for the many who would ask if they thought it was a possibility. Towards the end of the pregnancy the mother asked again, hesitantly. The head and another member of staff felt that the mother was tired and low in spirits, so it was agreed.

On another occasion, a white mother living in bed and breakfast accommodation had her daughter in a part-time place (there were no full-time places) when her baby boy was born. The baby was suspected of having a genetic disorder and had to be taken to various hospital appointments. The mother explained she might not be able to bring her daughter every day because she could not collect her at the end of the morning. The head offered to keep her daughter with her between the part-time sessions and have lunch with her. Every day that the baby went to hospital, and every day for the following three months that it took the family to adjust to the care their son needed, the head and Stacey lunched together.

We often expect children and parents to be able to make do with what is offered to the main group, whatever their circumstances. It sometimes appears that the degree of conformity can determine whether family or individual shall have access to the rewards available. The same can be true on a much wider scale. Patterns of speech and pronunciation, private/local authority schooling, income, where one lives, skin colour, religion, family history, marital status and sexual orientation – all give signals to others about whether people are in a favoured group or not. We all need to guard against our prejudices and misconceptions.

This is the problem with having one stated version of what the curriculum should contain; it is not flexible enough to incorporate the perspectives of different groups. An example of this is the insistence in the National Curriculum Key Stage 1 history syllabus on retaining the story of Guy Fawkes as part of our heritage. It is a heritage, but it is a debatable one. For instance, it is a different heritage depending on whether families are bringing up their children in the Catholic faith or as Protestants. Furthermore, for those with other faiths and those with none it must be hard to tell what message is intended to be taken from this story of religious conflict, political unrest, conspiracy, betrayal and judicial torture followed by a hideous death.

There are also individuals in society who are not able to build a viable life for all sorts of reasons including illness, domestic disasters, unemployment and so on. People in these situations need and deserve as much help as possible, and their children's rights to an appropriate education must be upheld with particular care. High standards are vital; it has been shown that children are by no means destined for a life of failure, even when their early lives are full of difficulties and deprivations. What they need was clearly identified by a study based at the National Children's Bureau (Pilling 1990). She showed that, of a group of children from the most disadvantaged backgrounds of all, some children succeeded to a marked extent in later life in spite of their early disadvantages. The parents of the successful ones retained high ambitions for them and spent time with them, playing with them, reading to them, taking them to the park. Practitioners can help if they can find ways to show their appreciation and support for the relationship between parent and child, and if they can contribute their own understanding of what the parent is trying to do. However, as it is quality of relationships that is the crucial factor, practitioner intervention needs to be very sensitive to family relationships and situations, and to cultural differences.

Security and love underlie personal and educational development

Parental confidence is the key to much of their children's success (Pugh *et al.* 1994). What helps children to make a success of their lives is the value of good child-rearing at every level of society, and practitioners should show awareness of this at every stage of education. This can happen as long as we recognize the importance of not having one rigid picture of good child-rearing practices; we have to be culturally adaptable and respectful, with criteria for effectiveness based on children's progress.

Practitioners and parents sharing intentions

A young father, Chris, is pleased that his daughter Christina has made a smooth transition into the infant school from the nursery class. He and his wife have been teaching her to recognize her letters. The teacher has asked them not to use upper case only, but to show her lower case when it is appropriate. This is quite a surprise for the parents; they had assumed that they would start with all one kind of letter because it was easier, and that capitals were best because of the way that shop signs and names on packets of food are so often in capitals.

Chris is willing to follow the teacher's request, however. He appreciates that she has been trained in how to teach and that there will be differences between the way he and she see things. While his daughter was settling into the nursery class he noticed that there was little direct teaching going on, and a lot of learning through play. He says 'It wasn't the way I thought, at first, but now my wife has explained that the children are supposed to learn through doing, I can see the way the school is thinking.'

But there are also things that happen at home that would change the way the teacher sees this little girl, if she knew about them. For instance, Chris is bilingual; he was born in Greece and speaks Greek with his parents and family friends. He would very much like to pass this inheritance on to his daughter, but he worries about her having to learn a language she cannot use in her daily life. 'There's a Saturday school attached to the church where my father goes . . . My mates try to teach their kids, but when I try and talk to them they don't seem to want to answer. One of them told me it was dead boring, and she didn't see the point of it.'

Even if there was no other way to give support, the teacher could show her interest in Christina having a bilingual parent and be sure to include Greek in the languages and scripts available in the classroom. There might be other things she could do to help, like telling Greek stories among the folk tales and fairy-tales, and asking Christina to teach the other children Greek words for familiar people and objects.

Some might wonder how much difference it would make if the teacher knew about Chris's wish to teach Christina Greek. With all the other things she has to do, is it a good use of her time? Two significant aspects are:

1 Understanding of this part of the relationship between Christina and her father and grandfather is helpful at times when the teacher, Mrs S., wants to make a particular effort to help Christina feel at home in the classroom. It can also help with Christina's understanding of others who are or are not able to speak more than one language.
2 Sharing this part of their home life will help Chris and his wife feel more 'in tune' with Mrs S., and will make them feel that their perspectives on Christina are valued.

But the sharing of intentions and perspectives between parents and practitioners is not easy in a busy classroom. There has to be a rationale for it, and it needs links with a curriculum model which sets a value on children's experiences at home with family and friends. It requires just as much commitment as sharing intentions with children does.

In a DAC, contacts with the home are seen as a part of the curriculum, and a part of the practitioner's responsibility to provide for children's learning in ways that suit them. The first step is to consider what kind of contact with parents is most valuable, and to find out what kind of contact with the setting is needed by parents.

We have begun with practitioners' wishes for contact because there is a lot of work that may have to be done on their side before contacts, however much wished for, can be successful. Practitioners need to establish in themselves what they believe about home-setting partnership and how important they think contacts with parents are for their work. They also need to think about how to overcome barriers that may be causing some parents to hold back. Comments such as 'these parents wouldn't really understand' show that sometimes practitioners feel completely out of their depth in relating to parents; this can happen for all sorts of reasons and is a definite sign that something is going very wrong. Similarly, 'You only see the parents of the good children – you never see the ones you really want to see' is a warning that the children who most need help are getting the least. Somehow barriers must be overcome, and differences made into a source of strength.

In the early years, home and community culture are extremely influential on learning and children do not leave their culture behind them as they come in through the doors of the setting. This gives practitioners the challenge of planning a curriculum that embraces children's culture and draws on its strengths. Perhaps the most demanding task practitioners face is to make links for children between their current understanding and knowledge and the more advanced learning that the practitioner wishes them to progress to. We have described already the difficulties presented by a curriculum which seeks to be standardized and is therefore not able to reflect the experiences and cultures of minority groups. A curriculum with its aims set out in broader and more flexible terms would make it easier for early years practitioners to draw in all their children. However, it is also the task of the practitioner to be flexible and creative in interpreting the requirements of the existing curriculum and adapting it to children's circumstances. Nothing makes the case for well-educated practitioners more obvious. In the end, it is the quality of practitioners' understanding of the nature of the different subject disciplines that determines how well they do this, just as it is the quality of their understanding of child development and of the children as individuals that determines how they construct and implement the curriculum as a whole so as to give all children the opportunities for learning that they need.

Practitioners need to know the children and to understand enough of their cultures to be able to construct an appropriate curriculum. This is where they gain one great benefit from contacts with parents, and where the parents also have much to gain since, while practitioners are learning what they need to know, they are also sharing information about how they work, which is invaluable to parents when they help their children at home. However, for these contacts to take place, time is needed, whether for home visits or for conferences in the setting. A setting following a DAC will be able to allocate time for parents and practitioners to talk together because the educational value of these contacts is clear. The setting will gain from sharing such concerns as:

I worry about underestimating children when they are so young and come from a great range of different backgrounds and experiences.

I need their help with monitoring progress.

I can learn a great deal from the parents, who have known the child from birth.

The closer the partnership the more consistency of handling for the child – we can share our intentions for children's behaviour.

The child needs to feel secure, that parents and practitioners are working together.

Parents need to know what goes on in the setting in order not to be panicked by political or media manipulation.

It helps parents to make judgements about the quality of what is provided by the setting if they have real experience of what happens in their child's class or group.

Parents have a lot to offer to the setting; not just any special talent, but just as ordinary supportive adults who will tell or read a story, chat to children, help with puzzles, share games and work with children generally.

Practitioners may not be the victims of society's prejudices against particular groups, yet they may be resistant to sharing their professional domain with parents. Practitioners may be understandably concerned about encroachments on their area of responsibility. The meaning of professionalism is that you have an area of expertise which is acknowledged as being highly specialized, and rightly so. Lawyers, doctors and architects are in the same position. All professionals have to ask themselves two questions:

1 To what extent is it right for me to share my specialized knowledge, for which I received many years of training by experts? Would it weaken or

dangerously undermine the real value and meaning of this knowledge if I shared a small area of it with those who did not have access to an informed starting point?

2 If it *is* right, to what extent can I convey this knowledge to others in such a way that they can use it to make informed decisions for themselves or their children?

In the case of practitioners, it is appropriate to explain and share as much as possible because it is best for the child, who is their professional responsibility. Unlike a lawyer, they depend on the parents of their 'client' to support their professional intentions. But it is not easy to explain all the professional issues, and we have to help practitioners to become better able to articulate their work to parents and others.

But these are not the only issues at stake. There is a question which is even more important and which should come before the others. The care and education of young children is personally sensitive. As in many other professions, early years practitioners need to have good ongoing relationships with the families (parents and children) and a constant flow of communication between themselves and parents. How is this to be fostered and shaped to include what both sides need to share and to know? There is much information that practitioners can only have access to through parents, and they need practical ways in which to learn it – occasions for easy exchanges of view. It is important also that parents share just as much as they feel able to; practitioners must be careful not to exercise pressure or push people in directions that are not suitable or even possible for them. Conversely, practitioners need to be able to hear and understand parents' communications when they do happen, and it may be personally quite challenging to respond appropriately.

The following example illustrates both the nature of the partnership between practitioners and parents, and how a structure based on respect for the parent–child relationship can support it.

The nature of partnership in education in the early years

Life is one long transition for the under-6s; if parents do not offer constant well-informed support, who else can do this job? Sometimes parents are in serious trouble and need support themselves. The setting can help them and be a kind of buffer area for parent and child without turning the relationship into a social-work one. Sensitivity and self-awareness are essential for this (Whalley 1994: 28–33).

Adam was 5 when his parents parted, after some very painful months. Soon his mother was dealing with his sense of rejection, his anger and his grief. His outbursts were hard to contain, and his behaviour deteriorated in other ways too, becoming very distractible and aimless. His mother asked his teacher whether he showed any signs of disturbance at school, but apparently there were none. She felt that the teacher and headteacher did not understand how serious the problem was; the head told her that a firm hand was all he needed. After a few days with no improvement she sought help through her GP and was referred to a local hospital's child guidance clinic. Gradually, Adam's behaviour at home improved. It therefore came as a bombshell to learn a few weeks later that the school was now experiencing the same behaviour that had so concerned her, and that if it did not improve they felt that they would have to exclude the child. His level of achievement had dropped, and he was falling behind the other children in his work. His mother did her best to get Adam to behave at school, and somehow he came through the behaviour difficulties in the end, but she felt very let down by the way the problem had been handled. She felt strongly that if the school had taken Adam's difficulties seriously when she first reported them there could have been a joint approach instead of a fragmented one which seemed to give him little sense of consistency and prolonged his unhappiness. It had also caused him to miss several months of his schooling and to have a sense of himself as a failure. Over a year later she was oppressed by a sense that Adam had been failed when he most needed help.

Ways and means

Children and parents can go through very difficult times together in the early years, and practitioners can do much to help or hinder them. How can we help practitioners to help parents? We have to recognize that practitioners need proper training, and they need a pedagogy that accepts the importance of understanding children's development. At present, the model of the curriculum that practitioners have to work with does not do this, and the training of intending teachers marginalizes child development and assigns the role of customer to parents. It is to be hoped that before long, a new understanding of the care and education of such young and emotionally vulnerable children will permit practitioners to work with the support of a curriculum that is founded on child development theory as well as on subject knowledge.

Then, perhaps, intending teachers will have time in their courses for developmental approaches to learning, and for sessions and practical experience devoted to how to work side by side with parents. Perhaps this will help them to understand the experiences that all parents share, whatever their culture, and to find ways to assign equal importance to the developmental concerns of each child and family in spite of the great differences that there are between them.

Something to think further about

We have to help practitioners to help parents, but there is another side as well; we need to make it easier for parents to communicate with practitioners. How might home visiting help?

7

The way forward

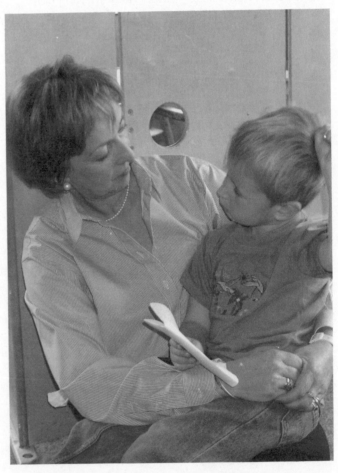

Mutual respect and concern lead to self-confidence and trust

In the light of what we have been saying in earlier chapters, it must be clear that some fundamental and radical changes must be made if we are to offer children the educational opportunities which will equip them to lead their future lives in purposeful and fruitful ways. These changes are long overdue. As long ago as 1965 a memorandum to the Plowden Committee stated, 'I believe there is now a new and very strong psychological case for the root and branch re-thinking – and eventual reconstruction – of our whole scheme of primary education.' The writer, Nathan Isaacs, went on to say that any changes would have to be in accordance with the educational principles which 'are, in substance, simply those of the great educational reformers from Rousseau to John Dewey, viz, the education of children through their own live interests, activities and first hand experiences' (Isaacs 1965 :1).

The Plowden Report took note of what people like Isaacs were saying, and initiated important changes in the way we talk and think about primary and early years education. Teacher education courses devoted a considerable amount of time to the study of child development, and classrooms and curricula began to be organized in ways which would encourage the kind of self-initiated, self-directed and self-motivated learning which, as we have outlined, is intrinsic to a developmentally appropriate approach. It is a matter of the deepest concern that this development, which was the subject of well-argued and innovative thinking and practice, did not take root.

We look back on this period as a short but fruitful age in early education which sparked off many promising educational ideas and practices which were worthy of further development. Our primary schools became the envy of the Western world, and were visited and fêted and emulated by many, especially in the USA. However, it was indeed a short period. In 1969, a backlash against 'progressive' methods was spearheaded by the infamous 'Black Papers '(Cox and Dyson 1969), in which they stated that 'It is our belief that disastrous mistakes are being made in modern education, and that an urgent reappraisal is required of the assumptions on which "progressive" ideas, now in the ascendant, are based' (p. 6). Angus Maude, in his contribution, said, 'Taking a long view, one must conclude that the most serious danger facing Britain is the threat to the quality of education at all levels. *The motive force behind this threat is the ideology of egalitarianism*' (Cox and Dyson 1969: 7; our emphasis). Concern for the achievement of quality of learning thus became associated with a political antagonism to a genuinely democratic educational philosophy. In turn, this led to an antagonism towards developmental approaches. The Black Papers and their blanket and doctrinaire 'debunking' of these methods, which were based on an understanding of young children's needs and capabilities, created an anxiety in the general public which led to a serious undermining of innovative approaches. They also created a suspicion of educational theory which has continued to be a marked feature of educational policy making.

However, the professionals in education continued to draw on the well-thought-out pedagogy from which Isaacs spoke. They clung to their professional conviction that the learner's self-motivation and direction make for the best learning, and this has continued throughout any subsequent modifications which, over the years, have been deemed to be appropriate; that is, until the introduction of the Education Reform Act and the National Curriculum in 1988. It is this Act, and its programme of attainment targets, key stages, testing and circumscribed content, that reinforces our call for change. There has been a strong move away from the research evidence and ideas which are the basis of early childhood education. It is not just the ramifications of the Act itself which have created a need for change in schools and other educational settings. Simultaneously, there have been moves by the State towards more adult direction; more 'whole class' approaches; more testing at younger and younger ages; more pressure for schools to admit children as young as 4 into reception classes; more demand for a return to so-called 'traditional' methods of schooling; and more attacking of practitioners who do not wish to succumb to these pressures. The result has not only been to undermine practitioners, especially those working with the youngest children, but to turn the education system in a backward direction. Kelly (Blenkin and Kelly 1994: 1) sums it up:

> . . . educationists from other countries do not now visit the UK to study its approaches to early education, or to primary education generally, because these have reverted to being no different from, and certainly no longer superior to, their own. And, in explaining why they do not now do so, they express incredulity and amazement at the disappearance, indeed the destruction, of a system which was once their envy. And, further, they evince great concern that current policies in the UK reflect not only a rejection of what they see as significant advances which had been occurring there, but also movement in a direction which is the complete reverse of the directions of development to be seen in their own countries. There is a groundswell of contrary movement throughout Europe.

How, then, to bring about the changes which we believe to be necessary if we are to return to providing education which truly meets the needs and abilities of our young children? We consider this both from within the setting and from outside it.

Within the setting

If we are to become more effective, we have to start with ourselves

We have to recognize that we are responsible for our own professional development and growth. 'Outside' bodies like local education authorities can assist with this, but the impetus must come from us. Crucially, change comes from within ourselves. We have to be prepared to look at ourselves objectively, and reflect on our practice with open-mindedness and whole-heartedness and with the courage to actually make changes when we recognize that they need to be made. This can be greatly assisted if we work in conjunction and genuine consultation with our colleagues, observing each other in friendly partnership, for the improvement of tech-niques, attitudes, styles of interaction and so on. We first have to accept that *we* are the ones who probably need to change, before we can make appropriate classroom/setting changes.

What strategies can we use within settings to gain insight into our own practice?

In Chapter 1 we discussed the importance of practitioners having a sound pedagogical basis on which to build their educational practice. We believe that reasserting and revisiting pedagogy, updating our knowledge and understanding of how children learn, and of their developmental needs and capabilities, is a first important step. 'As long as the profession con-tinues to argue that teaching quality arises from personality traits, rather than from the consistent application of pedagogic theory, teaching effec-tively for understanding rather than for knowledge transmission will remain an elusive goal' (Galton 1997: 115). We have shown throughout this book that, in spite of the current denials of it, the bulk of the research and experience in early childhood substantiates the principle that curriculum design should spring from consideration of the ways in which children learn. This implies, for example, that the more we can organize and plan our education so that we work with children on a one-to-one basis, and in small groups rather than with the class as a whole, the more we will suc-ceed in our educational aims. So, steeping ourselves in the study of teach-ing and learning will give us the knowledge and understanding which will support us in upholding what we genuinely believe is right for chil-dren. In this way, we can start to measure our own practice against what we have been studying, and begin to modify it where we see fit. Changing ourselves is one of the hardest things to do, but it can also be exciting and revitalizing, especially if we do not try to go too fast, but alter things bit by bit. Change is not only an event, it is also a process.

Refreshing ourselves in this way means we will also need to reconsider our own values and beliefs, and be aware of their implications for our teaching. This may involve becoming more self-aware, and reassessing our own self-knowledge, which can help us to see the relationship between ourselves and our role as teachers. And then, we must add the *willingness* to change. The Quality in Diversity framework emphasizes this.

> The fundamental purpose of the framework is to ensure quality in the educational experiences of children from birth to eight. This purpose can only be realized through the conscientious work of early childhood practitioners: both in their daily work, face to face with children, and in their development work, when they deliberately structure opportunities for themselves to think about their work and learn from one another.
>
> (ECEF 1997: 83–4)

We need to stand back from ourselves and try to be objective about our attitudes and styles of teaching; to be prepared to reappraise what we are doing, and to what extent we are truly achieving our objectives; to be prepared to allow colleagues to observe us, and to share and discuss their insights as openly as possible, within a framework of mutual professional trust.

Apart from looking to ourselves, of course, we might, for example, also want to question aspects of the National Curriculum, or to challenge patently silly notions such as the idea that class size does not affect the quality of our teaching. The courage of our convictions gives us the strength to do this.

There are many ways in which we can set about replenishing our knowledge and understanding:

- taking full- or part-time courses is an obvious way, but is not always the easiest to achieve;
- undertaking one's own research, albeit in a small way, can give insights of inestimable value into whichever aspects of educational issues and practice one is examining.

Investigation, preferably in collaboration with colleagues, into work within one's own setting, has been shown to give an exciting impetus to practitioners' new thinking and practice. This is because it is very focused on one's own work, is containable, is immediately relevant, and involves a cycle of reflection about oneself and one's work which should lead to improved practice. Although he was talking about teachers, what Kitson so neatly says also applies to all practitioners: 'Effective teachers need to be reflective teachers' (Kitson and Merry 1997: 136). There are currently three major projects in the UK which are concerned with promoting such investigation, and which are already having a considerable effect on practitioners working in various types of setting, whether voluntary, state-maintained or private.

1 The Quality in Diversity Project has already been discussed in Chapter 2, and quoted above. Suffice it to say here that the numerous suggestions for ways in which practitioners can 'further each other's learning' (ECEF 1997: 83) emanated from the very practitioners who themselves had taken part in evolving the Framework.

2 The Principles into Practice (PiP) Project, directed by Geva Blenkin at Goldsmiths College (1993–7), also engaged in finding ways of improving the quality of children's learning, and one aspect focused on the professional development of practitioners working in the early years. In the latter, case-study, part of the project, practitioners chose their own focus for their researches, using action research approaches to improve their practice and understanding. In the first phase of the project (1994), apart from gaining evidence about the qualifications, resources and nature of provision for young children in group settings, the views of early years practitioners on what they believe constitutes quality provision were collected (Blenkin and Kelly 1997). We refer to some of these findings later. Phase 2 is more relevant to the present discussion, because it involves practitioners in action research into aspects of their own practice, and includes people from all kinds of settings (Blenkin and Yue 1994). The project report quotes examples from practitioners who have been working in this way:

> The research has taken my thinking on to a higher level (reception teacher);
>
> It has given me a morale boost, built my confidence as a practitioner and, I feel, has made me a more productive member of staff (nursery nurse);
>
> Instead of just putting things out, we now say – why are we putting that out and what are the children gaining from it (nursery nurse);
>
> Doing action research has revitalized my interest in children's learning and I feel more fulfilled and in control of my teaching (reception teacher).

3 The Effective Early Learning Research Project (EEL) is also concerned to find ways of making early years practice more effective. Again,

practitioners from all over Great Britain, in differing settings, have been involved in considering their own practice and, as a team within their situation, have followed a process of evaluation and development during which they have evolved strategies to bring about change and more effectiveness. Apart from making time to observe the children at specific intervals, in order more precisely to identify their needs and capabilities, one of the strengths of the project has been the way in which practitioners have found the courage to observe each other, and so to gain valuable insights into their own and others' strengths and weaknesses. As a result,

> . . . evidence is emerging that practitioners who have been working with the EEL methodology are empowered by the process. Taking responsibility for evaluating their practices, being given the tools to undertake this, and the means to move their practice on, has given the practitioners a sense of self worth and control over their professional lives. They report higher self esteem, and a growing belief in the importance and complexity of their work.
>
> (Pascal and Bertram 1997: 49)

A second strategy is fine-tuning our analytic, evaluative, observational and communication skills. These are intrinsic to what we have been saying, and the three projects referred to above all offer strategies and techniques for achieving this. In Chapter 5 we discussed, in some depth, the question of observation and its importance for adult learning. Observation is often neglected in the areas of creativity in all its aspects (music, dance, the 'plastic' arts etc); in the area of social and emotional development; in the area of outdoor activities, where both physical and imaginative capacities can flourish; and in the (generally undervalued) area of spiritual development, where a sense of wonder, especially about the natural environment, needs to be nourished.

A third strategy is working together as a team, sharing ideas and expertise, planning and organizing together in a democratic way. This is not only more likely to make for shared and agreed aims, but makes it easier for colleagues to be more open with each other, to come to trust each other, and so be able to help each other for the ultimate benefit of the children.

The above strategies will in themselves lead practitioners to rethink the following:

The need to plan and organize for more opportunities to work with children both in small groups and on a one-to-one basis
The younger the children, the more they need this kind of intimate, individual help and attention. Practitioners themselves gain much knowledge

and understanding of children from being able to converse and share ideas and negotiate plans in this way. The children's sense of security and well-being is much enhanced, leading to their becoming more successful learners. Moreover, organizing the programme in this way makes life much easier for the practitioner, who can move more peacefully from group to group, and/or child to child, making use in a more economical way of his/her time and expertise.

The need to pay particular attention to the 4-year-olds (and, indeed, 3-year-olds in some areas of the country), especially those unfortunate enough to find themselves in reception classes

As we said in our introduction (pp. 6–7), we believe that the majority of 4-year-olds in this country are being done a serious disservice, and very likely being harmed both psychologically and educationally, by being catapulted into reception classes before they are anywhere near ready. Their parents and carers, teachers and governors are encouraged to let them slip through the nursery net (where they should be) by renaming them as 'younger 5s', or 'rising 5s', or 'other 4s' or indeed 'rising 4s'. But they are 4 in their own right, and should be regarded and treated as such. So practitioners (and parents) must remind themselves that 4-year-olds need to be actively exploring their world; to have plenty of space to move about in; to have time to express themselves verbally and to pursue and complete activities in comfort; to be able to play in self-directed and self-initiated ways; to have opportunities to experiment with a large variety of creative materials; and to be encouraged to represent their thoughts and ideas in their own inimitable fashion. (It should be added that although we are talking here about the 4-year-olds, we believe that these needs apply equally to children from birth to 6.)

The need to plan and organize for more opportunities for children to play, both indoors and outdoors

This is especially important in reception classes, where children, and especially the 4-year-olds, are so often being denied this right. This will mean having ratios of at least 1:13, and will involve sharing the intentions of practitioners and children alike, and planning much of the activities together. This does not exclude the fact that practitioners will have certain aims for children which are important to fulfil; merely that they will be achieved in ways which more appropriately match children's interests and ways of learning. Working in this way may well mean actually altering the layout of the available space so that children can move about more freely, and so that the adults can also have more opportunity to move from child to child, and small group to small group. This in itself means that the adult

will have a better chance of getting to know his/her children more intimately, understand their strengths and/or difficulties, and establish closer
relationships with them.

The fact of being able to work more with individual children is vitally
important, as it means we can be more learner-centred, so helping children
to move forward in their thinking. It also means that there is more possibility of ensuring that all aspects of children's development – social,
emotional, communicative, physical and intellectual – can be planned and
catered for. It is especially important to pay attention to the emotional
well-being of the child. This is an area of development which is often
neglected, and yet it is of great significance for the ways in which children
will progress. Laevers (1991: 5) regards the child's emotional well-being as
one of the most conclusive indicators of quality education:

> The degree of well-being shows us how much the educational
> environment succeeds in helping the child to feel at home; to be
> her/himself; to remain in contact with her/himself, and have her/his
> emotional needs (for attention, recognition, competence) fulfilled.

We know from our own experience that anxiety, insecurity and stress
can seriously undermine what we want to do – it is extremely difficult, for
instance, to work or study when such emotions are flooding through us.
But we regain our zest and determination and drive when we have a sense
of being at ease with ourselves, confident and secure in the feeling that we
can achieve what we want. It is, of course, the same with children, and we
need to be aware that they may be under-functioning because of some
emotional problem which is gnawing at them.

All the above points, of course, apply equally to indoor and outdoor
learning. The outdoor learning environment is an undervalued aspect of
children's lives, and having the opportunity to play outside is often misunderstood to be simply a time when children can storm around the
playground 'letting off steam'. But it can and should be more than that. It
is part of the whole educational experience, and as such, needs careful
planning and supervision. Outdoor areas need thoughtful landscaping,
with a mixture of grassy and hard surfaces; with trees (preferably
climbable) and shrubs; with a garden area where children can create and
maintain a garden of their own; with perhaps a pond or a wild flower
area, where children can observe and care for animals and insects. The
usual climbing frames, slides and so on should be there, as well as large
toys with wheels, mats, hoops, barrels, balancing forms and so on. In
other words, when children are outside, there should be every opportunity for them to enjoy what should be an extension of their adventure
in education.

The need to develop closer partnerships between the setting and the parents or carers of the children

The beginnings of a trusting relationship between home and setting can be established as soon as the child's name is put on the waiting list. The more the setting shares its aims with parents, and gives them the opportunities to observe the children and staff at work, the more consistent will be the approach to the child, making for a better sense of security and of understanding parameters of acceptable behaviour. Ways and means of involving parents are numerous – inviting them to help with certain tasks with the children in their setting; offering talks for parents on different aspects of child development, or of children's learning; home visits by the staff (which can greatly help to establish trust between adult and adult, and between child and adult); encouraging parents to share their concerns with staff, in discussions on a one-to-one basis; inviting parent governors (where present) to spend time in the setting, observing the daily programme so that they come to understand more of the general approach to education which the setting holds.

So much for the kinds of change which might be made within settings themselves.

What changes need to be made 'outside' early years settings?

The education of teachers and other practitioners

In recent years, the move to involving schools, to a far greater extent, in the training of student teachers means that students will inevitably model themselves on the teachers they encounter. This means that only very limited changes are likely to take place in both styles and general approaches to teaching, making for a more static and less innovative profession. Many teachers, too, are either uncomfortable with having to take on the extra duty of being responsible for such a large part of a student's training; or in all honesty they are not very good at it, having, perhaps, a lack of confidence in themselves as successful teachers. At the same time, the amount and type of educational theory which is undertaken at universities and colleges has been much diminished. We believe the balance between theory and practice needs to be redressed – practitioners must have a theoretical base from which to make decisions about how and what to teach.

This leads us to the content of the courses which early years practitioners undertake. One of the most serious and retrograde steps which teacher education institutions have had to take in recent years, has been to virtually eliminate the study of child development. It seems to us quite bizarre that student teachers are expected to initiate young children into various subjects, and to see to their social and emotional needs, without having any understanding of how children learn, or of their different intellectual capacities and capabilities at different stages of development. There have been numerous complaints from students and teachers about this. Amongst the initial findings of the PiP project, for example (Blenkin and Yue 1994), it was found that the majority of heads of every type of group setting, whether located in the voluntary or state-maintained sector, ranked *Knowledge of child development* as the single most influential factor in the professional development of practitioners who work with the under-8s; and knowledge of school subjects was placed relatively low. We believe child development should have a core place in courses, both at initial level and in PGCE and similar courses. If it were to be reinstated, our new young teachers would not only start off with a much sounder grounding in how to set about their task, but would also have had the opportunity to become the self-aware people we discussed earlier. Interestingly enough, courses for nursery nurses, playgroup workers and childminders, as well as NVQ and BTEC students, all have a core of child development running through them.

More opportunities to study child development in in-service courses would also be of great value for continued professional development (CPD). This applies equally to teachers, childminders, nursery nurses, playgroup leaders and any other practitioners in charge of the welfare and education of our young children.

Whilst there are many more courses now available, such as NVQs at different levels, there is at the same time a move away from four-year teacher education degree courses, to three-year courses. This not only goes against the mainstream developments in the rest of Europe and elsewhere, but is a retrograde step in itself. If we acknowledge that teaching is a highly skilled profession, needing a breadth of knowledge and understanding of children, of subject matter, and of teaching techniques, then we must also recognize that a considerable amount of time is needed to master these different facets. Four years is the minimum length necessary.

The establishment of a General Teaching Council or similar body

This would help to ensure that there was not only more consistency amongst education courses across the board, but that a single body would be able to monitor, and be responsible for, all matters to do with teaching. This would bring about much more coherence for the whole of the teaching profession.

Last but not least

All practitioners working with young children need to be more forceful and articulate in fighting for what they believe is in the best interests of children. People working in early years education have seldom been granted the status which they deserve, nor the recognition of the highly important contribution which they make to the education of our children and, through this, to society as a whole. Moreover, because they have been reticent in standing up for themselves and their beliefs, they have remained as the Cinderellas of the profession, being regarded as having little to offer in the way of what the public considers 'proper' education.

If this is to be changed in any positive way, early years practitioners must be prepared to articulate their concerns and beliefs. This takes courage and conviction, but we believe that what we have offered in this book will help to make this possible.

Bibliography

Barrett, G. (1986) *Starting School: An Evaluation of the Experience*. Norwich: AMMA.

Bettleheim, B. (1975) *The Uses of Enchantment*. London: Thames and Hudson.

Blenkin, G. and Kelly, A. V. (1994) *The National Curriculum and Early Learning: An Evaluation*. London: Paul Chapman.

Blenkin, G. and Kelly, A.V. (eds) (1996) *Early Childhood Education: A Developmental Curriculum*, 2nd edn. London: Paul Chapman.

Blenkin, G. and Kelly, A.V. (eds) (1997) *Principles into Practice in Early Childhood Education*. London: Paul Chapman.

Blenkin, G. and Yue, N.L. (1994) *Principles into Practice: Improving the Quality of Children's Early Learning (Year One: June 1993–May 1994) – Interim Report*. London: Goldsmiths College.

Bowlby, J. (1969) *Attachment (Vol. 1): Attachment and Loss*. London: Penguin.

Bredekamp, S. (1987) *Developmentally Appropriate Practice in Early Childhood Programs Serving Children from Birth through Age 8*. Washington DC: National Association for the Education of Young Children.

Brierley, J. (1988) *Long Shadows in Childhood: A Case for Nursery Education*. London: British Association for Early Childhood Education.

British Association for Early Childhood Education (1994) *Our Present is Their Future: Quality in Early Childhood Education* (videotape). London: BAECE.

Bruce, T. (1991) *Time to Play in Early Childhood Education*. London: Hodder and Stoughton.

Bruner, J.S. (1974) *Beyond the Information Given*. London: Allen and Unwin.

Bruner, J.S. (1977) *The Process of Education*. Cambridge: Harvard Education Press.

Bruner, J.S. (1983) *In Search of Mind*. New York: Harper and Row.

Bruner, J.S., Jolly, A. and Sylva, K. (eds) (1976) *Play: Its Role in Development and Evolution*. Harmondsworth: Penguin.

Carey, J. (1997) Spinner of Yarns under the Palms, *Guardian Education*, 22 April, p. 5.

Carnegie Corporation of New York (1994) *Starting Points: Meeting the Needs of our Youngest Children*. New York: Carnegie Corporation.

Cleave, S., Jowett, S. and Bate, M. (1982) *And So to School: A Study of Continuity from Pre-school to Infant School*. Berkshire: NFER-Nelson.

Cox, C.B. and Dyson, A.E. (1969) *Fight for Education: A Black Paper*. London: The Critical Quarterly Society.

Department for Education (1993) *Initial Training of Primary School Teachers. Draft Circular*. London: HMSO.

Department for Education (1993) *Statistical Bulletin: 11/93*. London: HMSO.

Department of Education and Science (1988) *The Education Reform Act*. London: HMSO.

Department of Education and Science (1989) *The Implementation of the National Curriculum in Primary Schools*. London: HMSO.

Dweck, C.S. and Leggett, E.L. (1988) A social-cognitive approach to motivation and personality. *Psychological Review*, 95, No. 2: 256–73.

Early Childhood Education Forum (ECEF) (1997) *Quality in Diversity in Early Learning: A Framework for Early Childhood Practitioners*, draft version. London: National Children's Bureau.

Egan, K. (1988) *Primary Understanding*. New York: Routledge.

Egoff, S., Stubbs, G.T. and Ashley, L.F. (eds) (1980) *Only Connect: Readings on Children's Literature*. Canada: Oxford University Press.

Erikson, E. (1963) *Childhood and Society*. New York: Norton.

Fox, C. (1993) *At the Very Edge of the Forest: The Influence of Literature on Storytelling by Children*. London: Cassell.

Froebel, F. (1887) *The Education of Man*. London: Edward Arnold.

Fromm, E. (1966) *The Fear of Freedom*. London: Routledge.

Galton, M. (1997) Primary culture and classroom teaching: the learning relationship in context, in N. Kitson and R. Merry (eds) *Teaching in the Primary School: A Learning Relationship*. London: Routledge.

Garvey, C. (1977) Play, in J. Bruner, M. Cole and B. Lloyd (eds) *The Developing Child Series*. London: Collins/Fontana Open Books.

Goldschmied, E. and Jackson, S. (1994) *People under Three*. London: Routledge.

Guha, M. (1996) Play in school, in G. Blenkin and A.V. Kelly (eds) *Early Childhood Education: A Developmental Curriculum*, second edition. London: Paul Chapman.

Hohmann, M., Banet, B. and Weikart, D.P. (1979) *Young Children in Action: A Manual for Preschool Educators*. Ypsilanti, MI: Highscope Press.

Hurst, V. (1997) *Planning for Early Learning*, second edition. London: Paul Chapman.

Hutt, C. (1966) Exploration and play in children. *Symposium of the Zoological Society of London*, 18: 61–81.

Isaacs, N. (1965) Memorandum for the Plowden Committee. *Froebel Journal*, 2: 12–33.

Isaacs, S. (1960) *Intellectual Growth in Young Children*. London: Routledge and Kegan Paul.

Joseph, J. (1993) 4 year olds in school: cause for concern, in P. Gammage and J. Meighan (eds) *Early Childhood Education: Taking Stock*. Derby: Education Now Publishing Cooperative.

Kitson, N. and Merry, R. (1997) *Teaching in the Primary School: A Learning Relationship*. London: Routledge.

Laevers, F. (1991) *The Innovative Project 'Experiential Education' and the Definition of Quality in Education*. Belgium: Katholieke Universiteit of Leuven.

Lawlor, S. (1994) *Nursery Choices: The Right Way to Pre-school Education*. Policy Study No. 140. London: Centre for Policy Studies.

Lee, L. (1964) *Cider with Rosie*. Harmondsworth: Penguin Books.

Marshall, S.P. (1997) Does education and training get in the way of learning? *RSA Journal*, CXLV, 5477, March.

Miller, L., Rustin, M., Rustin, M. and Shuttleworth, J. (eds) (1989) *Closely Observed Infants*. London: Duckworth.

Navarra, J.G. (1955) *The Growth of Scientific Concepts in the Young Child*. New York: Teachers College, Columbia University.

Paley, V. (1981) *Wally's Stories: Conversations in the Kindergarten*. Cambridge, Mass.: Harvard University Press.

Pascal, C. and Bertram, T. (1997) *Effective Early Learning Research Project*. Worcester College of Higher Education.

Pellegrini, A.D. (1991) *Applied Child Study: A Developmental Approach*. Hillsdale, NJ: Lawrence Erlbaum.

Piaget, J. (1962) *Play, Dreams and Imitation in Childhood*. London: Routlege and Kegan Paul.

Piaget, J. (1966) *The Origins of Intelligence in the Child*. London: Routledge and Kegan Paul.

Pilling, D. (1990) *Escape from Disadvantage*. Lewes: Falmer.

Principles into Practice (PiP) Project. (1994) *Improving the Quality of Children's Early Learning (Year 1: June 1993–May 1994): Interim Report: 1995*. London: Goldsmiths College.

Pugh, G., De' Ath, E. and Smith, C. (1994) *Confident Parents, Confident Children*. London: National Children's Bureau.

Rogers, C.R. (1974) *On Becoming a Person*. London: Constable.

Rosen, B. (1988) *And None of it was Nonsense*. London: Mary Glasgow.

School Curriculum and Assessment Authority (SCAA) (1996) *Nursery Education: Desirable Outcomes for Children's Learning on Entering Compulsory Education*. London: DfEE.

Smilansky, S. (1980) *The Effects of Socio-dramatic Play on Disadvantaged Pre-school Children*. New York: John Wiley.

Tizard, B. and Hughes, M. (1984) *Young Children's Learning, Talking and Thinking at Home and at School*. London: Fontana.

Trevarthen, C. (1993) *Playing into Reality: Conversations with the Infant Communicator*. Winnicott Studies, No. 7, Spring 1993: 67–84. London: Karnak Books Ltd.

Trevarthen, C. (1994) 'How children learn before school,' text of lecture given on 2 November 1994 at Newcastle University for BAECE.

Vygotsky, L.S. (1962) *Thought and Language*. Cambridge, Mass.: MIT Press.

Vygotsky, L.S. (1978) *Mind in Society: The Development of Higher Psychological Processes*. Cambridge, Mass.: Harvard University Press.

Wells, G. (1987) *The Meaning Makers*. Sevenoaks: Hodder and Stoughton.

Whalley, M. (1994) *Learning to be Strong: Setting up a Neighbourhood Service for Under-Fives and their Families*. London: Hodder and Stoughton.

Whitehead, M. (1996) *The Development of Language and Literacy*. London: Hodder and Stoughton.

Zipes, P. (1995) *Creative Storytelling: Building Community, Changing Lives*. New York: Routledge.

Index

STARTING FROM THE CHILD?
TEACHING AND LEARNING FROM 4 TO 8

Julie Fisher

Early years practitioners currently face a number of dilemmas when planning an education for young children. The imposition of an external curriculum seems to work in opposition to the principles of planning experiences which start from the child. Does this mean that the notion of a curriculum centred on the needs and interests of children is now more rhetoric than reality?

In a practical and realistic way *Starting from the Child?* examines a range of theories about young children as learners and the implications of these theories for classroom practice. Julie Fisher acknowledges the competence of young children when they arrive at school, the importance of building on their early successes and the critical role of adults who understand the individual and idiosyncratic ways of young learners. The book addresses the key issues of planning and assessment, explores the place of talk and play in the classroom and examines the role of the teacher in keeping a balance between the demands of the curriculum and the learning needs of the child.

This is essential reading, not only for early years practitioners, but for all those who manage and make decisions about early learning.

Contents
Competent young learners – Conversations and observations – Planning for learning – The role of the teacher – Encouraging independence – Collaboration and cooperation – The place of play – The negotiated classroom – Planning, doing and reviewing – Evaluation and assessment – References – Index.

192pp   0 335 19556 3 (Paperback)   0 335 19557 1 (Hardback)